WARRIOR • 131

NELSON'S OFFICERS AND MIDSHIPMEN

GREGORY FREMONT-BARNES   ILLUSTRATED BY STEVE NOON

Series editors Marcus Cowper and Nikolai Bogdanovic

First published in 2009 by Osprey Publishing

Midland House, West Way, Botley, Oxford OX2 0PH, UK

443 Park Avenue South, New York, NY 10016, USA

E-mail: info@ospreypublishing.com

ISBN: 978 1 84603 379 7

E-Book ISBN: 978 1 84603 903 4

Editorial by Ilios Publishing Ltd, Oxford, UK (www.iliospublishing.com)

Page layout by: PDQ Digital Media Solutions Ltd, Bungay, Suffolk

Index by Auriol Griffith-Jones

Typeset in Sabon and Myriad Pro

Originated by PDQ Digital Media Solutions Ltd, Bungay, Suffolk

Printed in China through Worldprint Ltd

09 10 11 12   12 10 9 8 7 6 5 4 3 2 1

A CIP catalogue record for this book is available from the British Library.

FOR A CATALOGUE OF ALL BOOKS PUBLISHED BY OSPREY MILITARY AND AVIATION PLEASE CONTACT:

NORTH AMERICA
Osprey Direct, c/o Random House Distribution Center, 400 Hahn Road, Westminster, MD 21157
Email: uscustomerservice@ospreypublishing.com

ALL OTHER REGIONS
Osprey Direct, The Book Service Ltd, Distribution Centre, Colchester Road, Frating Green, Colchester, Essex, CO7 7DW
E-mail: customerservice@ospreypublishing.com

www.ospreypublishing.com

DEDICATION

This book is dedicated to my younger son, Monty, who, being fleet of foot and filled with a sense of adventure would have made an ideal powder monkey.

ARTIST'S NOTE

Readers may care to note that the original paintings from which the colour plates in this book were prepared are available for private sale. All reproduction copyright whatsoever is retained by the Publishers. All enquiries should be addressed to:

Steve Noon, 50 Colchester Avenue, Penylan, Cardiff, CF23 9BP, UK

The Publishers regret that they can enter into no correspondence upon this matter.

THE WOODLAND TRUST

Osprey Publishing are supporting the Woodland Trust, the UK's leading woodland conservation charity, by funding the dedication of trees.

CONTENTS

NELSON'S OFFICERS AND MIDSHIPMEN

INTRODUCTION

In the course of the French Revolutionary and Napoleonic Wars (1793–1815) and the Anglo-American War (1812–15), officers of the Royal Navy came to rank amongst the most respected members of British society, a consequence of their extraordinary record of leadership over the course of two decades of conflict against a host of adversaries, including the French, Spanish, Dutch, Danes and Americans. Whereas the Army had always been regarded as a suitable place for an aristocrat's son, this was not so in the Navy until the mid-18th century. Younger sons tended to join the church, Parliament or seek employment in the law, since the eldest son inherited the family estate. Thus, the Navy was a natural option for such young men, together with the sons of the growing middle class. Unlike in the Army, where commissions were attained by purchase, a high degree of professional skill was required in the Navy. As a consequence, naval officers and midshipmen were nearly always more competent and professional than their Army counterparts, and, since money played considerably less of a part in the process of promotion, the Navy naturally attracted men from a wider social background than the Army. Such men – who attained in the course of a generation a status not enjoyed either before or since – form the study of this short work, which will focus on their training, uniforms and equipment, daily life, pay, responsibilities aboard ship and experiences in and out of battle.

A young man seeking a Navy commission, before going to sea as a midshipman, might spend a short time at the Royal Naval Academy at Portsmouth, though educational standards were indifferent, and most of what he learned he acquired at sea under the tutelage of the ship's schoolmaster or chaplain, who received extra pay for tutoring a boy for one or two hours a day, usually in mathematics and navigational skills. The young lad usually spent six years at sea before sitting the lieutenant's exam at the age of 20 or more. If he passed, he received a commission and began the long climb up the promotional ladder, a process that could be accelerated by deaths at sea from sickness, disease or battle, or from the process of patronage that, notwithstanding the inability to purchase a commission or command, nevertheless rendered the Navy far from egalitarian. If he passed the exam for lieutenant – and a vacancy existed – he might receive an independent command aboard a sloop or brig, before eventually reaching the lofty rank of captain, which entitled him to command a frigate and, after further years of good service or connections, perhaps a ship of the line.

Nelson falls mortally wounded on the quarterdeck of the *Victory* at Trafalgar. Marines and Captain Hardy come to his aid, while in the centre foreground a midshipman takes aim at a French marksman in the rigging of the *Redoutable,* which lay to starboard. (National Maritime Museum)

The captain's range of responsibilities extended from the ship herself to the entire crew. He oversaw everything from the maintenance of discipline and hygiene to the allocation of food and accommodation. He not only possessed the authority to promote or punish, but in fact wielded more power than the king himself, for while a captain could order a man to be flogged, his sovereign could not. It was the captain who decided when and where battle should be joined – thus placing in his hands the power of life and death over the ship's company. In exchange for all these rights and responsibilities, he regularly risked his own reputation and life, with compensation in the form of higher pay, a greater proportion of any prize money than his subordinates and quarters of greater extent than those of all his lieutenants combined. In most cases he held his crew's respect, which manifested itself by high morale, skilled seamanship, a high standard of gunnery and a willingness to exert and sacrifice themselves for the captain, quite apart from king and country, as Admiral Sir Robert Calder recalled of his time as a ship's captain:

> When I commanded a single ship it was my chief delight to have the goodwill of my men, and I can safely assert ev'ry man under my orders would freely lay down their life to obey me or my commands, and by such means I made my crew both love and fear me. They loved me for my humanity and fear'd to cause my displeasure, and this I found the best school for seamen. They will fight for you and if required die for you.

A captain of this description – together with others possessing fewer virtues but greater connections with those of influence – might, if fortune served him well and infirmity and death eluded him, achieve a foothold on the ladder of promotion, up which greasy pole he would painstakingly negotiate his way from rear to vice, to full admiral, commanding as he went a squadron of half a dozen ships of the line or perhaps a fleet of 20 or more.

CHRONOLOGY

1793   The French Revolutionary Wars having begun the previous year, Britain joins Austria and Prussia in opposing France, bringing the full power of the Royal Navy to bear at sea while the Allies fight on land (1 February).

1794   In the first fleet action of the war, Admiral Lord Howe defeats the French off Ushant (1 June).

1795   Spain abandons the First Coalition and concludes a treaty of alliance with France against Britain, throwing her substantial fleet into the scales and forcing the Royal Navy to abandon the Mediterranean (19 August).

1797   Admiral Sir John Jervis vanquishes the Spanish at St Vincent (14 February), while the Channel Fleet defeats a Dutch force at Camperdown (11 October). Serious mutinies break out at Spithead (16 April) and the Nore (12 May) affecting the Channel and North Sea fleets, respectively.

1798   After fruitlessly searching the Mediterranean for the French fleet conveying Bonaparte's army to Egypt, Nelson finally discovers it anchored in Aboukir Bay, near Alexandria, where he annihilates it, leaving the French stranded without hope of reinforcement or withdrawal (1–2 August).

1801   Seeking to oppose neutral powers' limitations on British naval and commercial access to the Baltic Sea, the Admiralty dispatches a naval force to confront the Danish Fleet, which Nelson, albeit at significant loss to his own force, drubs at Copenhagen (2 April).

1802   After a decade of conflict in Europe, a fragile peace is established by the Treaty of Amiens, bringing an end to the French Revolutionary Wars (30 March).

1803   After French interference in the internal affairs of Switzerland and Holland, Britain refuses to evacuate Malta, as agreed at Amiens, as a counterweight to growing French hegemony on the Continent. Her declaration of war inaugurates a new series of conflicts known as the Napoleonic Wars (18 May).

1804   Irritated by Spain's ostensible neutrality but partiality toward France, Britain seizes a Spanish treasure fleet bound from Montevideo, provoking a declaration of war from Madrid (12 December).

1805   In the most decisive naval encounter in history, Nelson confronts a combined French and Spanish fleet off Cape Trafalgar, capturing or destroying over half the enemy's force and thus safeguarding Britain from invasion for the remainder of the war (21 October).

1812   After many years' deteriorating relations between Britain and the United States over maritime rights, open hostilities break out, requiring the Royal Navy to deploy substantial numbers of frigates and smaller vessels to the western Atlantic (18 June).

1814   The Allies capture Paris (30 March), bringing an end to hostilities.

1815   Having escaped from exile on Elba, Napoleon marches into Belgium where he is decisively defeated by the Anglo-Allied and Prussian armies at Waterloo (18 June). The Anglo-American War formally comes to an end in February, the as yet unratified peace having been signed at Ghent the previous Christmas Eve.

George Elphinstone, Admiral Viscount Keith (1746–1823). His numerous posts included Commander-in-Chief of the Mediterranean Fleet during the British expedition to Egypt in 1801, when relations with his captains became strained. (Author's collection)

TRAINING, PROMOTION AND APPEARANCE

Training and promotion

Midshipmen

Midshipmen, or 'young gentlemen', generally came aboard as a result of the patronage of the ship's captain, and therefore owed their appointment to what contemporaries called 'interest'. For the most part, a captain took on such boys for the sake of his own relations, to pay off a debt or to seek favour with an influential family, usually one with connections to the Admiralty. In choosing a midshipman a captain did not have to obtain the approval of the Admiralty; nor did the decision cost him anything, since he made no pledge to teach the boy navigation or seamanship. Such skills were to be acquired over time in his role as a sort of naval apprentice. Boys were put forward by families either who genuinely regarded a naval career as a worthy pursuit for their son,

A midshipman off to sea. One of a series of satirical cartoons by Cruikshank, tracing the career of Master William Blockhead of HMS *Hellfire*. The boy, oblivious to the realities of life at sea, torments his sister with a dirk while his mother weeps at his imminent departure and his father examines the enormous list of clothing and provisions, the bills for which stand piled high on the table. (National Maritime Museum)

or simply by those who found other professions unpalatable. Thus, those aspiring to hold command were not the products of families whose wealth alone could secure for them a commission (which, in any event, could only be acquired by purchase in the Army, not in the Navy), but boys prepared to rise through hard work and skill amidst a degree of squalor and discomfort. Oddly enough, though they might eventually reach the rank of admiral and command a fleet, or sit on the Admiralty Board and make decisions on naval strategy, there existed no formal method of selection for midshipmen. They came aboard at the behest of the captain, with the sole qualification being their connection – usually through family ties – with the captain, and thus they joined the Navy with not the least bit of ceremony or remark by the Admiralty.

A boy joined as a 'first-class volunteer', according to which designation he had to serve two years before he was made a full midshipman. If, on the other hand, he had already spent two years at the Naval Academy at Gosport, near Portsmouth, he could join his vessel as a midshipman from the start. During the 1790s, a boy could begin his service at sea from the age of 11, or perhaps a year or two younger, but in 1812 the minimum age was altered to 13, with the exception of officers' sons, who could come aboard at the age of 11. In terms of numbers, a first-rate ship carried 24 midshipmen, a second-rate had 18, a third-rate, 12, and fourth- and fifth-rates fewer according to their size.

Instruction in navigation, nautical astronomy, and trigonometry was given every morning to midshipmen from 9am until noon by a schoolmaster, who was also expected to ensure that his pupils maintained as high a moral tone as possible under the circumstances and to report to the captain any boy whose attitude towards his work gave cause for concern. In almost all cases, the schoolmaster was also the ship's chaplain, paid for his tutelage out of the pupil's wages. Where neither a chaplain nor a schoolmaster served aboard the ship, the captain taught the midshipmen himself, sometimes denying them their meal until they could establish the ship's position by dead reckoning or by the altitude of the sun.

Once a boy reached the age of 15, and was properly rated a midshipman, he became known as an 'oldster', with concomitant higher pay, a cessation of lessons by the schoolmaster and a proportion of daily grog allotted to him. From this point he moved from the gun room into the midshipmen's berth on the orlop deck, situated in the after cockpit, where he messed (ate) with older midshipmen who had passed their exams and qualified as lieutenants, but were merely awaiting promotion, as well as with the master's mates. After two years' further service he was eligible to sit the examination for master's mate, if he wished to be qualified to pilot prize vessels into port, so long as he could demonstrate competence in navigation and seamanship.

From 1794, in order to be eligible for promotion, a midshipman had to have reached the age of 19 and acquired a certain amount of 'sea time', which meant that he had to possess a certificate confirming that he had been on the ship's books for at least six years, two of which spent as a midshipman or master's mate, to be able to sit the examination for lieutenant before the Navy Board examiners or a quorum of three sea captains. The system was open to fraud, however, for an unscrupulous captain, usually seeking some favour from the boy's parents – who might have influence at the Admiralty, for instance – could place a boy's name in the muster book for a year or two before the boy actually went to sea, therefore providing him with unearned 'sea time'. But from 1794 the captain could not carry on this activity with such disregard for the consequences, for in that year volunteers began to receive pay, and if a boy's name appeared in the muster book, then the Navy Board necessarily dispensed funds which, if the captain kept (for, after all, there was no boy to receive this pay), he was committing fraud, with the resulting court martial putting a swift end to his career.

Although regulations barred a midshipman from becoming a lieutenant until he was 19, in an age when birth certificates were not issued in a standard fashion, ways of circumventing the system easily existed, such as the creation of forgeries by bribing a parson or local worthy. A birth certificate, forged or otherwise, when produced with certificates (themselves legitimate or illegitimate) supplied by captains who claimed the lad had at least six years of sea service under his belt, enabled a midshipman to clear the first hurdle of his naval career. According to William Falconer, author of the much-respected contemporary naval reference work, *Universal Dictionary of the Marine*, captains' testimonial were to attest to the boys' having been not only 'diligent and attentive to the duties of their profession, but [having] at all times been obedient to the commands of their superior officers'.

The second step, of course, required a midshipman to pass the examination, which, while originally only possible in London before the Navy Board, eventually could be conducted by three senior captains at one of the main ports, such as Portsmouth or Plymouth, or if abroad by the station commander-in-chief ordering his three senior captains to establish a panel of examiners. These reforms spared the candidate the potentially great inconvenience and expense of having to reach London. In the course of his examination the midshipman's fitness came under scrutiny rather more closely than the documents he brought, which could not, they appreciated, with any degree of reliability prove his age

A midshipman carrying his journal and sextant, by Thomas Rowlandson, 1799. (Stratford Archive)

Prince William Henry (later William IV) who, though a midshipman a decade before the French Revolutionary Wars, is shown here wearing the uniform that remained in standard use throughout the 1790s. (Stratford Archive)

or the number of years he had served at sea. That is not to say that every midshipman sat the exam as soon as he reached 19; it all depended on how much 'sea time' he had accumulated, and at what age he had come aboard. James Gardner, the son of a captain, was 25 when he sat his lieutenant's exam, having spent 13 years as a midshipman.

If a boy possessed a sound understanding of seamanship and navigation that usually sufficed to persuade the examining board of his fitness for a commission. If he failed to answer satisfactorily a battery of questions, the midshipman would have to apply again a few months later. Some tried innumerable times and never succeeded, remaining midshipmen for years or even decades. Whereas the admirals and captains who composed the board were perhaps less than exacting in investigating a boy's age, they were not inclined to promote a boy who could not meet the important responsibilities of a lieutenant, for the ship herself and the lives of her crew might rest on his decisions – good or bad. A young man might succeed by sheer luck, with the board neglecting to test him on his perhaps imperfect understanding of astronomy or mathematics, but if he appeared to be strong in matters navigational, or otherwise exhibited virtues connected with leadership and strength of character, that was usually sufficient. There was no medical examination, which was just as well for the likes of those of a weak constitution like Horatio Nelson.

Even when he passed his exam, a midshipman might not in fact receive a commission, for without a vacancy in a ship he could go nowhere, which meant that he joined the collection of disillusioned young and middle-aged men who had 'passed for lieutenant', yet continued to make their home in the midshipmen's berth for an indeterminate period. There were 2,000 such men in this situation in 1813, having served their time and passed their exams but with no vacancy to fill. In these cases, they sometimes accepted a post as a warrant officer, but if in this capacity they subsequently found their ship decommissioned (what contemporaries called being placed 'in ordinary'), they did not, like commissioned officers, receive half pay.

If a midshipman passed his exam and received his commission – with or without a ship to receive him – he at least now, unlike his status as a midshipman, had an official existence, with his name added to the Sea Officers List, the forerunner of the Navy List, and he became eligible for half pay in the event that he could find no employment. Even if he passed the board, however, he still faced anxiety over his seagoing appointment, for while some might bring excitement, action – and thus the likelihood of more rapid promotion through distinguished conduct or the death of an officer – and possibly even prize money, others could be boring and carry little prospect of advancement. Determination of an appointment was usually influenced by one's record of service as a midshipman and any connections one possessed within influential naval circles.

Lieutenants, captains and admirals

A newly created lieutenant began his commissioned years at the bottom of a list, so that as men higher up the list died or were made commanders or post captains, his name would move up the list, with new names added beneath his. This did not necessarily mean, however, that he had to wait his turn to be promoted in strict order of seniority, reaching the top of the lieutenants' list because of the death, retirement or promotion of men above him. Rather, to make 'commander' or 'post captain' was a process of selection, not a simple mark of longevity. Thus, a lieutenant at the top of the list could remain unselected for years – even decades – sometimes for the remainder of his life. In 1799, for instance, the lieutenant at the top of the list had had his name down since 1744 – that is to say, over half a century. The names of the two following were listed under '1747', the two after that as '1757', with another 14 under '1758'. Clearly, then, a lieutenant aspiring to a captaincy could 'jump the queue' over his peers, for patronage often played a role here as did meritorious conduct in action, as a result of which his captain might enter his name in the 'record of proceedings', thus increasing the young lieutenant's chances of promotion ahead of his less distinguished contemporaries. It is important to observe, however, that a lieutenant did not need to wait for promotion to command an unrated vessel, such as a cutter or gun boat, of his own, and could, in the event of the incapacity or death of her captain – but only temporarily until a new captain could be found – take charge of a fifth rate (a frigate of 32 to 44 guns) or sixth rate (a brig or sloop of 20 to 28 guns). Whatever the actual size or rate of the vessel, however, he was addressed as and referred to as 'captain'. While a lieutenant only commanded a sixth rate, a commander never served aboard a vessel smaller than a sixth rate.

Waiting Room at the Admiralty, where aspirants and petitioners of various sorts sought to apply, or plead their case, for an appointment, promotion or pension. While a man who reached the rank of captain often did so with at least some degree of 'influence' or 'patronage', that is not to say that the Admiralty was prepared to risk its ships in the hands of someone without the requisite skills to handle it properly. Thus, unlike in the Army, a naval officer could not purchase a commission. In short, the Admiralty would not knowingly allow an incompetent officer to reach the exalted position of captain. (Stratford Archive)

A newly appointed lieutenant admires himself in the mirror as his gleeful family and the household servants look on. Note the telltale single epaulette, stockings, decorated cocked hat and straight sword that betray his new commission. (Stratford Archive)

For a lieutenant seeking a captaincy in the strict definition of the term, appointment to a ship would come in the form of a sixth-rate ship, a promotion which made him in the early years of the war a 'master and commander', later simplified to 'commander'. On the other hand, it was possible for a skilful and brave lieutenant to skip this rank and move straight to command a fifth rate, particularly if he were the first (i.e. senior) lieutenant of a flagship (the ship in a squadron or fleet aboard which an admiral flew his flag) and enjoyed the favour of that admiral. Thus, if a captain of a frigate in such a squadron or fleet died, a popular lieutenant stood a good chance of filling his shoes without occupying the intermediate role of commander. This was particularly so for men posted to the West Indies, where the chances of survival were poorer than in European waters owing to the prevalence of a host of deadly tropical diseases.

 A

LIEUTENANT AND MIDSHIPMEN: UNIFORMS, WEAPONS AND PERSONAL EFFECTS

Lieutenants (**1**) wore a blue coat with white piping on the lapels, three buttons with one row of white piping on the cuffs, blue collar with white piping and no epaulettes. From 1812, lieutenants wore a single plain epaulette on the right shoulder, while commanders wore two, also plain, but with bullion around the edges. Sub-lieutenants, a rank introduced in 1804, were dressed as lieutenants, while midshipmen had no lapels, three buttons on their cuffs, a blue collar with white collar patch and no epaulettes. A lieutenant often carried a swagger stick (**2**) and employed a speaking trumpet (**3**) to make himself better heard, especially when addressing men aloft or amidst the cacophony of battle. His personal weaponry always included a sword (**4**), of which this example is an officer's hanger (a short, curved sword) of 1805 carried in a leather and brass scabbard. In a logbook (**5**) a lieutenant recorded information on the daily proceedings of the ship, such as course, position, speed, weather and any events deemed worthy of notice. The lieutenant's sextant (**6**) and quadrant (**7**) enabled him to determine latitude and longitude, the ship's course and the distance she covered in a 24-hour period.

When in uniform, a midshipman, shown here in the styles of 1797 (**8**) and c.1812 (**9**), carried a dirk (**10**), hanger or full-length sword (**11**), particularly if he were no longer an adolescent. Both lieutenants and midshipmen carried a pistol (**12**) in boarding actions, with fine black powder held in a flask (**13**), though in combat, with little or no time to reload, the ball-shaped butt of the weapon could be used as a club – hence its brass cup.

Admiral Samuel Hood, first Viscount Hood (1724–1816), who distinguished himself in the Mediterranean in the 1790s, particularly at the siege of Toulon in 1793. Nelson remarked that he was 'the best Officer, take him altogether, that England has to boast of … equally great in all situations which an Admiral can be placed in'. (Author's collection)

A captain commanded a single vessel of war rated from a fifth rate – designated a 'post' ship, with the senior officer no longer designated 'commander' but 'post captain' – to a ship of the line mounting between 64 and 120 guns. Most began their captaincy in command of a frigate, whose captains were generally regarded as particularly bold, for they sought promotion to a two- or three-decker and, as such, were sometimes prepared to take extraordinary risks in battle. If an admiral did not require such captains for scouting or work in charge of repeating frigates, then the latter could continue cruising, seeking both prize money and fame. In short, command of a frigate was sought after as an important step in the ladder of promotion to senior command.

While a captain might serve ten years in command of a frigate before being considered for promotion to a 50- or 60-gun ship as preparation for eventual command of the largest classes of warship, in some cases he went straight from a frigate command to that of a third-rate vessel, mounting 74 guns. However, a commander who was 'made post' had no guarantee of further promotion, for if his ship was decommissioned and there was no vacancy aboard another frigate, the post captain could not revert to being a commander, but rather went on half pay, retaining the rank of post captain – a position he could conceivably occupy for the rest of his life if patronage and a vacancy did not ease his path upwards.

Once an officer reached post rank he was bound, in the course of time, to become an admiral by sheer dint of seniority. A man who became a midshipman at 12, for instance, lieutenant at 20 and captain at 28 – whether or not thereafter he stood on half pay or on active service – remained on the Sea Officers List, so that as men above him died or were promoted, he inexorably moved up in their stead. Once he reached the top of the captains' list, he became a rear admiral upon the next promotion above him which created the necessary vacancy, now putting him at the bottom of the rear-admirals' list and setting him on course to move slowly up through the three categories of rear admiral, three of vice admiral and three of admiral. Thus, whereas lieutenants lower down on the list could be selected as post captain ahead of others, captains did not jump the queue to reach the rank of admiral.

Appearance

Midshipmen wore their hair short in the style of ordinary seamen and thus did not braid it into a queue. Uniforms for midshipmen were not standardized, but generally consisted of a blue tail-coat lined with white silk, the front ornamented with small gold anchor-buttons, with a white patch, called a turn back, on the collar. He wore white breeches and a waistcoat. His hat bore some resemblance to the top hat that would gain popularity during the Regency period (1811–20). Around his neck he wore a black silk handkerchief, his shoes were black leather and his shirts were made of frilled white linen. For foul weather the midshipman wore a glazed hat, watch-coat, and a waistcoat, often scarlet. While all such articles were associated with midshipmen, in reality his dress, purchased privately by his parents, varied both in style and quality and according to prevailing fashion and thus did not technically constitute a uniform.

Lord Nelson in the full dress uniform of a vice admiral. At Trafalgar he wore a flag officer's undress uniform and for reasons unknown left his sword in his cabin. The uniform in which he was mortally wounded, still extant, is now in the National Maritime Museum, Greenwich. (Stratford Archive)

Once a midshipman's garments had worn out or were stolen, he had to purchase clothes from the slop (garment) chest or continue to wear his threadbare clothes. This was generally acceptable, for hard service at sea led some captains to ignore the untidy or even slovenly look of such boys, whose appearance was not necessarily considered worthy of correction or punishment. Of course, if a midshipman received an invitation from his captain to dine, the young man made what attempts he could to smarten himself up, borrowing cleaner or better-quality items of clothing from his mates in the berth. In battle he might wear his dirtiest outfit, whereas when on boat service he tended to dress with greater care, lest he impugn the honour of the ship when the craft reached shore and came into public view.

When war broke out in 1793 officers were wearing the uniform introduced in 1787. The style for lieutenants and higher ranks was altered in 1795 – the most notable new features being the introduction of epaulettes – with a general degree of simplification, possibly because of economies due to the war, but more likely because civilian dress was becoming less elaborate in the 1790s as a result of the influence on fashion – even in Britain – of the French Revolution, which spurned the stockings, powdered hair, wigs and ornate coats associated with the aristocracy. When the Prince of Wales became Prince Regent in 1811 further changes came about in March 1812. While standard uniforms were issued, officers sometimes introduced changes of their own to reflect personal taste or exercised the (usually granted) privilege of retaining their old uniform until it wore out. Variations in dress also came about as a result of long cruises in which officers were unaware of changes to dress until they returned to a home port.

Two patterns of dress existed for officers: full dress, worn for ceremonial purposes, and undress. In the course of the wars the cut of the coat changed, as did its facings, the amount and quality of the braid and the style of the hat. Officers wore a cocked hat, which had evolved from the earlier 18th-century tricorne, with a brim higher in the back than the front, and worn in the early years of the wars 'athwartships'; that is to say, with the points extending out over the side of the head. Over the years, however, the hat was made with brims of equal size, and was worn 'fore-and-aft'; that is, with the ends facing forward and back, though admirals in full dress tended to wear their hats in the old style for a decade after the end of the Napoleonic Wars.

Without delving into the minutiae of undress uniform specifications, according to the regulations in force between 1795 and 1812, the coat of a captain of over three years' service in that rank was blue with an unlined lapel, plain cuffs with three buttons, a blue unlined collar and an epaulette on each shoulder. For captains with under three years' service, and commanders, the uniform was the same, except that the former wore only one epaulette – on the right shoulder – while a commander wore one epaulette on the left shoulder.

B **ADMIRALS AND CAPTAINS: UNIFORMS, WEAPONS AND PERSONAL EFFECTS**
The junior captain (**1**), commanding a frigate, wears a typical dress uniform of c.1810, with white pantaloons and black-tasselled Hessian boots. The single epaulette, as discussed, marks him out as a captain of less than three years' post. Beside him, this captain (**2**) in full dress uniform, c.1800, sports the finery as shown in the portrait of Captain Sir Edward Berry by John Singleton Copley, one of the period's foremost portraitists. The third captain (**3**) wears the 1795-pattern undress coat with closed lapels and the stand-and-fall collar characteristic of the Revolutionary Wars (1793–1802).

Figure **4** shows an admiral in undress uniform, c.1794, based on that dating back to 1787, with long lapels bearing 12 loops, extending as low as the upper edge of the pocket. Figure **5** shows an admiral in the regulation full dress uniform of 1795, still in use in 1805, with ten lapel loops and two cuff rings, though contemporary portraits show varying numbers of both of these. He wears medals on white ribbon, edged in blue, for services rendered at the battles of the First of June (1794) and for St Vincent (1797). Figure **6** shows Vice Admiral Nelson in the undress uniform he wore at Trafalgar, consisting of the 1795 regulation flag officers' undress, modified by an unlaced hat with a green shade which could be folded up or down to shield his damaged eye (a wound received in Corsica in 1794) from the sunlight. On his coat Nelson wore four embroidered stars: the Order of the Bath (top), the Order of St Ferdinand and of Merit (bestowed by the King of Naples, centre right), the Order of the Crescent (bestowed by the Sultan of Turkey, centre left) and the German Order of St Joachim (bottom).

Figure **7** shows a typical flintlock pistol carried by officers. Admirals and captains used telescopes (**8**) of varying design and length, all of brass and covered in black, brown or cranberry red leather. Senior officers took aboard what books (**9**) they could both for education and entertainment, sometimes compiling sizeable collections on navigation, seamanship, biography, philosophy and history. Captains' and admirals' swords (**10**, **11**, **12** and **13**) were not standard issue and thus varied according to taste, with weapons crafted to their own personal requirements and variation so diverse as to warrant a separate study of its own. Generally speaking, though, captains and admirals, in contrast to lieutenants and midshipmen, carried ornamented swords, with personal touches such as a pommel in the form of a lion's head and a flowing mane, nearly always in gilt metal, with ivory grips bound with wire and a plain knuckle guard in the shape of a stirrup. The blade, straight with a broad groove down its length, was often engraved with the royal cipher, masts, flags and anchors and occasionally decorated with a tassel of gold braid (**14**).

From 1812, all captains wore two epaulettes, but with the addition on the shoulder board of an anchor for newly appointed captains and a crown and anchor for those with over three years' service in that rank. The full dress uniform of a captain cost him more than his first quarter's pay, with the jacket and epaulette alone setting him back from 16 to 20 guineas, and the undress coat and epaulette eight guineas. A gold-laced hat cost another five guineas, and a sword and knot a further six guineas. A commander or post captain with less than three years' seniority wore only one epaulette, which rendered his coat somewhat less expensive, but the point remains that his income was insufficient to his needs.

CONDITIONS OF SERVICE

Food and accommodation

As was so often the case with boys going to sea with the object of becoming a midshipman, the reality of ship life seldom matched their expectations, as a newly arrived volunteer named Chamier discovered when he reached his new ship in port:

> I had anticipated a kind of elegant house with guns in the windows; an orderly set of men; in short, I expected to find a species of Grosvenor Place, floating around like Noah's Ark. Here were the tars of England rolling about casks, without jackets, shoes or stockings … the deck was dirty, slippery and wet; the smells abominable; the whole sight disgusting; and when I remarked [upon] the slovenly dress of the midshipmen, dressed in shabby round jackets, glazed hats, no gloves, and some without shoes, I forgot all the glory of Nelson, all the pride of the Navy, the terror of France, or the bulwark of Albion; and, for nearly the first time in my life, and I wish I could say it was the last, took the handkerchief from my pocket; covered my face and cried like the child I was.

A lieutenant, a figure who commanded the unquestioned obedience of the crew, especially in smaller vessels where he served as captain. (National Maritime Museum)

Up to the age of 15, midshipmen were known as 'youngsters'. These boys slung their hammocks in the gun room, with space extremely limited, as Chamier recalled in his memoirs: 'A hammock served as a bed, and so closely were we all stowed … that the side of one hammock always touched that of another; fourteen inches being declared quite sufficient space for one tired midshipman to sleep in.' They messed, in general, by themselves, under the watchful eye of the gunner, who looked after their clothes and generally saw to their material needs. In frigates they tended to eat in steerage, where their seniors messed.

The mess for older midshipmen was generally below the waterline, in the after cockpit, only partly lit and usually dingy and unpleasant. Lighting came in the form of a lantern and a thick glass scuttle, which allowed light into the ship's side. At best this space, from deck to beam, measured 1.7m, thus requiring men to remove their hats as they entered it, and many others still to stoop. An individual midshipman's berth was not usually larger than one square metre. Placed as it was, the midshipmen's berth had a foul atmosphere, for the bilges reeked beneath the orlop deck in a continual stench of

pestilence not duplicated anywhere else. This noisome environment was worsened by the odour emitted from the purser's storeroom, which contained rancid butter and putrid cheese, served out to the ship's company once or twice a week. Forward from their berth were the cable-tiers, where musty old rope was stored. While in most ships a windsail or ventilator led from the deck to the berth to provide the midshipmen with a modicum of fresh air, little could be done to relieve what was a generally oppressive and stifling environment in which to sleep, eat and entertain oneself.

Midshipmen had very little in the way of furniture in their mess. Certainly it contained a table, which doubled as a place at which to eat and as a surface on which the surgeon could carry out his essential services during and after battle. During mess times, the table was covered with a cloth or old hammock, on which, rather unhygienically, diners wiped their plate, knife and fork. The table was lit by tallow candles, stuck in beer or blacking bottles for safety. In the absence of chairs, which were not a regular feature of the mess, midshipmen used their chests. The berth contained no decorations on the ship's sides or on the bulkheads overhead; instead, various items such as clothing, boxing gloves, quadrants, hangers and other items were suspended on nails. In some cases, a locker contained their gear, plates, utensils and sea-stores, together with a container for a daily allowance of fresh water. A mess-boy was charged with keeping the berth clean, including the tablecloth, and was responsible for the cooking. Other servants for the midshipmen, known as 'hammock men', were either old sailors or Marines who lashed and stowed – and later carried down and unlashed – the midshipmen's hammocks in exchange for a glass of grog (rum diluted with water), paid each Saturday night. For additional grog or tobacco, servants occasionally washed the midshipmen's shirts while at sea. When in port, the midshipmen's linen and clothes were sent ashore to a washerwoman.

Midshipmen's berth, where the boys and men ate, studied and pursued various forms of entertainment. At night all its occupants slung their hammocks in the open space in the middle of the cockpit. (National Maritime Museum)

Elder midshipmen, the master's mates, the captain's clerk and sometimes the assistant surgeons also lived in the berth. Since some midshipmen, in practically all ships, were about 40 rather than in their younger years, and as many of the master's mates were of similar age, the berth was considered unsuitable for boys after dinner, not least when rum was available around 8pm. As such, the older men adopted the custom of sticking a fork in the table, or in the beams above it, as soon as the first watch was set. Once the fork was fixed in its place, the young mids immediately made for their hammocks, so that the place could be left to the older men, whose frequent use of unsavoury language betrayed those embittered by having been passed over for a lieutenancy. Those younger men who disregarded the custom after a second period of notice were struck with a knotted cord (known as a colt) or twisted handkerchiefs until they reached their hammocks.

It may readily be appreciated that a midshipmen's berth was not a place for the fainthearted; indeed, there was plenty of banter, horseplay, swearing and sometimes downright cruelty. Bullying was commonplace but considered one of the necessary evils of the place. Those who were not tough suffered for it: weak lads might have some of their food allowance taken off them, especially when they committed some misdemeanour, such as being late to night watch. A boy required a thick skin to survive under such conditions, and had to accept the total absence of privacy. Opportunities to read were infrequent and had to be snatched as and when time permitted. Fighting, quarrelling, fiddling, singing and general boisterous play was commonplace, and the captain seldom did much to restrain the mids so long as their activities did not interfere with the running of the ship. A sense of fairness and observance of the rules within the berth was largely absent, and apart from his food and sleep, the midshipman was not too fussed about life, as a result of which he frequently got himself into trouble.

The chief form of amusement in the midshipman's berth was card playing, with gambling officially banned yet widespread throughout the Navy. Much sport was also made of taunting those new to sea, especially when they suffered from seasickness. Pranks inflicted on such green hands included tying knots in his sheets, rigging his hammock so as to cause him to topple out, or stowing round shot and swabs under his blankets. Mischievous boys might also cut one of their colleagues down as he slept, hide his trousers in the galley oven, send him aloft for no useful purpose, dispatch him to find a sailor or Marine who did not exist, or involve him in other pointless yet amusing wheezes. Sending a young midshipman – after having rendered him drunk on rum – up on deck with a message for the officer of the watch, was almost certain to land him in hot water.

C **MIDSHIPMEN RELAXING IN THEIR BERTH**
In fifth rates and above, the midshipmen's berth was situated on the orlop deck, the lowest true deck in the ship, together with the surgeon's cockpit and the spirit room, and below which were the holds and ballast. A number of diversions were open to midshipmen when not on duty, including smoking (**1**), playing an instrument (**2**), reading (**3**) and writing home or in one's journal (**4**). In such cramped conditions, totally bereft of privacy, midshipmen were expected to wash, shave (**5**), dress and undress, eat and sleep, surrounded by the paraphernalia of life aboard ship: a lantern (**6**), sextant (**7**) and buckets (**8**) filled with sand or water to extinguish flames. Not shown is the vast array of personal effects required to 'fit out' a midshipman about to go to sea for the first time, whose parents were set back the hefty sum of from £70 to £80 for a home station or for service in the Channel, and from £90 to £100 for a foreign station. This included his entrance to the mess, which cost between £8 and £12, plus pocket money to cover his washing and other 'contingent expenses'.

Interior of a captain's cabin, which was situated in the upper stern of the ship, allowing the captain to emerge from his rooms directly on to the quarterdeck and straight to the steering position. His cabin was furnished according to his own personal taste. (Stratford Archive)

A midshipman's food was the same as that served to the men, consisting of such items as boiled pork or beef, bread, beer, oatmeal, butter, cheese, dried peas, local produce and biscuit, known as hard tack. Drink consisted of tea or cocoa when available, and invariably beer, or diluted wine or spirits, principally rum. Provisions officially furnished by the Navy were generally supplemented by purchases made in port by the caterer of the mess – usually a master's mate. Every member of the mess paid him between £3 and £5 on joining the ship, and about £1 a month while the ship was in commission. The caterer spent this money in a manner judged most suitable by him, but he generally stocked up on goods freely available in England, such as potatoes and onions, which were stowed in the lockers, or under the table, or in strings hanging from the beams. They tended to purchase Dutch cheeses whenever possible, along with coffee, tea, pepper and sugar. While in port the caterer sometimes bought bread and dried herrings. Beer was acquired whenever possible, but the regulation supply of Navy rum was quite sufficient for the needs of the men.

A midshipman was required to 'turn out' of his hammock at 7.30 every morning. Any hesitation – that is, failure to get on to his feet or 'show a leg' – instantly led to his being cut down and made to stand by force. Once roused, he washed himself in a little tin basin, which he balanced on the lid of his chest. He was expected to wash himself every day, unless fresh water was in short supply. He then dressed, blacked his boots or shoes, cleared away his bedding and stowed his hammock, leaving the breakfast table clear of soap, towels and blacking brushes. At 8am he had tea and biscuit for breakfast, or cocoa and porridge. At 9am he sat for lessons with the ship's schoolmaster.

Unlike midshipmen, officers lived in their own – albeit very confined – quarters. Cabin assignments varied according to rank: lieutenants, the master, the senior Royal Marine officer and the chaplain had cabins on either side of the wardroom, the largest cabin being reserved for the first lieutenant, who had access to one of the quarter galleys for his toilet; the other officers had to share the other quarter gallery. In frigates and smaller vessels, which did not have a wardroom, lieutenants lived in cabins on either side of the gun room on the lower deck. The captain lived in his own cabin, located at the stern of the ship. There he was destined to spend a good deal of time by himself – being captain was a largely solitary existence – though he would usually dine with some of his officers once or twice a week. Except aboard a ship of the line, the captain's cabin was rather cramped, yet nevertheless constituted one of the few places of privacy aboard a vessel crowded with men, guns and provisions. Admirals also had quarters at the stern of the ship, immediately above those of the captain.

Officers certainly ate better than the men, but hardly sumptuously, apart from their alcohol, which consisted of beer, spirits (chiefly brandy and gin), red and white wine, and fortified wine, such as sherry and port. According to the season they might also have punch or cordials. This is not to suggest that they remained in a permanent stupor, for they also drank tea, coffee and cocoa. Breakfast might include meat or fish, eggs, toast and marmalade; lunch (known as 'dinner') would be perhaps soup, fish pie, duck or pork and an assortment of vegetables such as cauliflower, carrots and boiled potatoes, and plum duff. The evening meal, known as 'supper', might consist of mutton, boiled duck with onions, roast goose, various types of fish, turnips, French beans, fruit fritters and apple pie, depending of course on the availability of the ingredients. Fish came either salted in barrels or caught fresh. Slaughtered livestock aboard the ship, in the form of chickens, ducks, sheep, pigs and cattle, provided the fresh meat so prominent on the officers' tables.

Pay and expenses

A midshipman's pay varied depending on the rating of the ship in which he served. Aboard a first rate, he received £2 15s 6d a month; aboard a third rate, £2 8s; aboard a sixth rate, only £2. A first-class volunteer received £9 a year, out of which was deducted £5 for the schoolmaster. Prior to 1794, he received nothing. A first-class volunteer or midshipman always found that his expenses exceeded his income, as a consequence of which it was essential that he should possess private means. For a volunteer, £30 or £40 per year was regarded as sufficient. For a midshipman this generally rose to £70–100 according to the relative cost of the station (e.g. Channel, North Sea or Mediterranean) on which his ship served. Men serving on foreign stations, where the exchange rate could be excessive, found their money of considerably lower value than those serving in home waters.

Whatever the sum owed, a midshipman did not even receive his pay until he had served a year at sea, and thereafter at six-month intervals. Falconer recommended that a midshipman's family or friends provide a newly appointed lad with between £30 and £50 per year – a sizeable sum at the time – to supplement his pay, in order to cover the cost of his clothes, mess and other expenses, and generally to allow him 'to appear at all times like a young gentleman'. To protect this sum from being lost, extravagantly spent or foolishly lent to unscrupulous members of the crew, it was thought best to present the boy's money to the captain for safekeeping, for if midshipmen managed it themselves, Falconer warned, it might 'be the means of leading them into every kind of vice and idleness when they get on shore, and can be of little use to them on board …'. If, however, a midshipman had to claim his pay in port rather than applying to the captain, he approached the commissioner sent to reside there by the Navy Board.

Until May 1806, the pay of a lieutenant depended on the rate of the ship in which he served, varying between 4s and 5s per day. The revised level of pay stood at 6s, regardless of the vessel's rate. A master and commander received

A contemporary cartoon lampooning the inequity of the prize money system. Here a sailor prays that the enemy's fire 'may be distributed in the same proportion as the prize money – the greatest part among the Officers'. Such criticism failed to recognize the fact that officers on the quarterdeck were exposed to greater danger than the crews manning the guns below decks. (Stratford Archive)

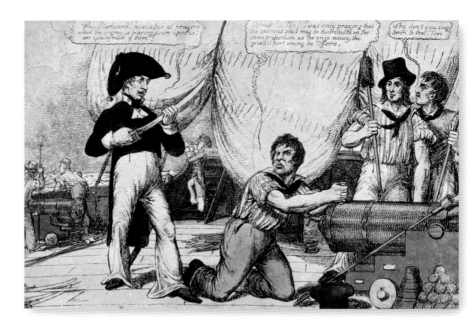

10s a day in 1806, while a captain's pay in the same year depended on the rate of the vessel he commanded, his income varying from 10s a day for a sixth rate to 24s a day for a first rate. If his ship were decommissioned he received half pay, what today would be termed unemployment benefit, based on a system of seniority. The first 30 men on the Sea Officers List (commercially available in a slightly different form as a small booklet called *Steel's Original and Correct List of the Royal Navy*) received 10s a day, the next 50 got 8s and the remainder 6s. So long as a captain swore an oath every six months that he was not in full employment on 'public service', he continued to receive half pay unless re-employed in the Navy or a branch of Government.

By contemporary standards a captain's pay was reasonably high, yet many became out of pocket very quickly, notwithstanding the fact that a captain – like everyone else aboard – was accommodated and fed at no charge. Other perquisites included, until 1794, the right to keep four servants for every 100 men aboard his ship, by which means he could provide for his friends and

D **CAPTAINS AND LIEUTENANTS SOCIALIZING IN THE WARDROOM**
Here the captain is assembled in the wardroom with three of his lieutenants in a relaxed atmosphere, the former having raised his glass to issue the standard light-hearted toast, which called not merely for victory, but a costly one – the better the opportunity for his ambitious subordinates to fill the shoes of their fallen superiors. The meal has not yet arrived; food for all hands was cooked on the iron stove in the galley, with that for the officers and warrant officers prepared on one side, and for the crew on the other. In a third rate or larger ship, the wardroom was located aft beneath the captain's cabin. In a three-decker (90 guns or more) this was on the upper deck, while in a two-decker (64–80 guns), the wardroom was on the lower deck. It was here that all commissioned officers and warrant officers with wardroom status ate and socialized. The position of the captain (**1**), shown here dressed in the style of about 1810, was a lonely one for he did not eat regularly with his lieutenants. Beside him sits a lieutenant (**2**) in undress uniform, c.1805, his coat fastened across, with white breeches and fashionable boots. Further along, sits another lieutenant (**3**) as he might have appeared in 1794, wearing an undress coat in blue, with lapels, plain cuffs and standing collar, together with skirts and pocket flaps, edged with white piping. The lapels have nine buttons, the cuffs and pockets three, with one button on the collar. His hat (**4**), resting on the table, bears a black ribbon and gold loop and button, in the 18th-century style of the tricorne. This was worn 'amidships' in the 1790s, gradually giving way, with the introduction of the flat bicorne (**5**), to the preference of wearing it 'fore-and-aft', i.e. with peaks to front and rear. The lieutenant standing (**6**) prefers modest dress, with a simple, unadorned black jacket and black Hessian boots instead of buckled shoes and stockings.

Vice Admiral Horatio Nelson and his ships' captains raise a toast in the wardroom of the *Elephant* on the eve of the battle of Copenhagen in April 1801. Note the midshipman on the extreme left. (Stratford Archive)

the poorer members of his immediate or distant family. Until the second year of the war, therefore, it was not uncommon for a captain to put to sea with a small group of parasites who followed him when he transferred to another ship, seeking promotion and other benefits on the basis of his generosity, good word and recommendations. To be a captain's servant did not mean that one functioned as a sort of flunkey, shining the captain's boots, serving his meals and arranging his clothes; rather, a boy entered the service under a captain's protection. Nelson himself began his life at sea as a 'captain's servant' to his uncle, Captain Maurice Suckling, but this by no means rendered him a mere steward, while Captain George Duff had his 11-year-old son aboard at Trafalgar. In 1794, when the system was finally abolished, a captain was compensated by way of a one-off payment, for until that time he enjoyed the privilege of removing from his ship, upon transfer, not only his servants, but his boat's crew, his coxswain, some of his warrant officers, his clerk and purser, and a number of able seamen. A captain of a first rate, for instance, could take with him 80 men, 65 from a second rate, 50 from a third rate, 40 from a fourth rate, 20 from a fifth rate and ten from a sixth rate.

If his pay did not always meet his expenses, the captain stood to receive a windfall in the form of prize money paid by an Admiralty court after a captured enemy vessel reached a home port – in his case, three-eighths of the value of the vessel. It was therefore quite natural that the prospect of prize money should stimulate his desire to close with the enemy as often as possible, provided of course that he perceived there to be a reasonable prospect of victory. Thus, expressions of hope for a decisive encounter with the enemy, followed by a lasting peace – and finally prize money – forms a common thread of captains' correspondence home on the eve of battle. Seldom, however, did captains come away genuinely rich as a consequence of prize money, but there were several notable examples, not least Lord Cochrane's remarkable success during a 13-month cruise against Spanish shipping in 1800–01, by the conclusion of which he had taken or retaken more than 50 vessels, 122 guns and 534 prisoners – an unprecedented scale of captures by a single ship captain.

Vice Admiral Adam, Viscount Duncan (1731–1804), the victor of the battle of Camperdown in October 1797. A deeply religious Scot with a reputation for coolness and courage, he was kind, unaffected and modest. (Author's collection)

Admirals received the highest rate of pay, depending on their position in the hierarchy of admirals, with rear admirals in 1806 receiving £1 18s 6d per day, vice admirals £2 5s 0d, and full admirals, regardless of colour, £3 17s 0d. Admirals also stood to receive a reasonable pension, as well, with those at the top of the scale, such as Lord St Vincent and Lord Duncan, victors of Cape St Vincent and Camperdown, respectively, receiving £3,000 per year, while even the most junior rear admiral received 5s a day. It was perfectly common, moreover, for admirals to remain on half pay for decades, into the late Victorian era, by which time they often died as vice or full admirals, notwithstanding the fact that their active service as captains may have ended in 1815, with the cessation of hostilities with France and the United States.

A midshipman being 'seized' to the shrouds as a punishment. (Royal Naval Museum)

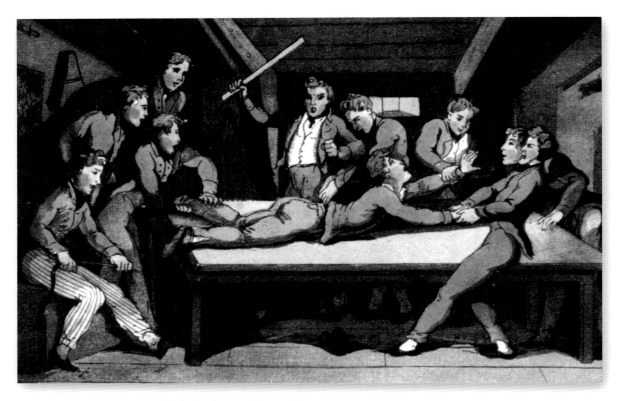

The senior midshipman administering punishment to an errant midshipman in the form of caning, c.1805. One of many images of shipboard life drawn by Thomas Rowlandson.

Discipline and punishment

A series of 35 statutes known collectively as the Articles of War formed the basis of naval law, by which transgressions were identified and punishments stipulated. It fell to the captain to read these out once a week to the assembled crew. Article 1 required that the captain hold church services on Sunday, while the remaining articles identified offences, to whom they applied and the various punishments at the disposal of a court martial. While nearly all the articles affected the whole of a ship's company, including its officers, a few applied

A midshipman mastheaded, one of a number of punishments meted out for minor acts of insubordination, laziness or other infractions.

particularly to them, such as Article 10 (cowardice), for which the penalty was either death or a punishment deemed suitable by the court martial; Article 15 (receiving a deserter), for which a commanding officer was to be cashiered; Article 17 (unauthorized receiving of property), for which officers were cashiered; Article 31 (failure to charge an offender), for which the court would levy a suitable punishment; and Article 32 (scandalous, or infamous behaviour), for which officers were dismissed from naval service.

Both midshipmen and officers handled disciplinary problems, the former on an informal basis, where enforcement of the rules aboard ship was dealt with on the spot without any requirement to consult with, or report to, an officer. Notwithstanding the youth of many midshipmen they possessed a considerable amount of authority, with license to bully and even maltreat any and all of those seamen subordinate to themselves, which amounted to most of the crew, all in the name of maintaining discipline. To oppose a midshipman could amount to mutiny; thus, if struck by a midshipman or abused with foul language for some oversight, a sailor simply had to grin and bear it. Indeed, midshipmen exercised nearly the same sort of power over the ordinary ratings as the officers, and did not hesitate to strike a man – whatever his age or size – with fist, leg or rope's end in answer to an infraction, real or imagined.

Midshipmen themselves were of course subject to naval discipline, which usually came in the form of mastheading, by which the mid was sent to the topmast or topgallant cross-trees to sit, rather uncomfortably, for several hours at a time. In the course of this period – sometimes for as long as 24 hours – he missed at least one meal, and depended on the topmen to supply him

Flogging. Monotony at sea – with long and tedious months of patrols and blockade duty – often drove men to heavy drinking, leaving a captain with frequent recourse to the lash to discourage drunkenness. Here one such officer listens to a plea for clemency from a sailor who, with shirt off, appears himself to be admitting to the crime, while a lieutenant and midshipmen stand on the captain's left and right, respectively. (Stratford Archive)

surreptitiously with meat and drink. When the ship happened to be in a warm climate, mastheading constituted a fairly mild punishment; indeed, many regarded it as rather a relief from duty. But in inclement weather the experience was most unpleasant. He might lash himself for safety to the cross-trees and get some sleep if the weather permitted it, and at night make his way silently and unobserved down the mast to the top, a wooden platform suspended high up the masts, there to sleep in somewhat greater comfort on the studding sails, informing the topmen of his whereabouts so that they could answer for him if he were hailed from the deck.

Yet more severe methods were also available to lieutenants for the punishment of midshipmen. The offender might be lashed or 'spread-eagled' in the weather rigging, approximately half a dozen ratlines above the hammock nettings. In this most uncomfortable position, the midshipman faced the wind, with his arms and legs widely stretched, causing him to become chilled for an hour or more, with the spray rising up periodically. This punishment, considerably more severe than mastheading, was usually inflicted for sleeping while on watch. For the same offence a midshipman might be dowsed, by which he was drenched with a bucketful of water poured from a height. Some captains took a more severe line, ordering the boatswain's mate to rig a grating in a cabin, and laying the midshipman either across the grating or over a gun, delivered a dozen strikes with a knotted rope's end, known as a colt. Indeed, few lieutenants or captains actually carried out corporal punishment themselves, preferring to leave this unseemly task to the boatswain or boatswain's mate. For taking a meal in the berth on the same day on which he had dined in the captain's cabin or wardroom, a midshipman was struck by a stocking filled with sand, or, as before, a knotted rope. Alternatively, he could be kept on deck after his watch was officially over. A midshipman might also be caned or 'started', which was effectively the same as receiving a blow from a colt, but he was not restrained.

In the case of a serious offence committed by any member of the crew, regardless of rank, recourse was always made to the captain, who would hear testimony by both accuser and accused, who could engage an officer to speak on his behalf if he wished. If a captain called a court martial, this body consisted of between five and 13 members. The procedure was similar to its civil equivalent on land, except that the members, who served in lieu of a jury, were all officers – hardly a trial by one's peers if the defendant happened to be an ordinary seaman. If the court martial found the accused guilty, flogging, sometimes with hundreds of lashes, could result. The most draconian form was 'flogging round the fleet', by which the convicted party was rowed to every ship in harbour and given a specified number of lashes – sometimes with fatal consequences. Such cases were, however, exceptional, and most captains ordered a punishment of a severity that did not require a court martial to sanction. There were a host of these, including disrating, stopping of grog and a restricted number of lashes; in theory he was only entitled to order 12 without referring the case to a court martial. An unscrupulous captain could, however, simply charge a man with several offences, thereby raising the number of lashes to 24 or more without referring the case to a tribunal. Some captains could be cruel and tyrannical, having frequent recourse to disproportionately severe punishment, though there were never many brutes of this sort. In a minority of cases, such men made the experience of the crews concerned a floating hell, bringing the crew to mutiny and causing the hanging of those responsible for the outbreak.

ON CAMPAIGN

Midshipmen and lieutenants

Midshipmen performed a myriad of tasks aboard ship. Having completed their lessons in navigation and other skills they went on deck, according to their respective watches, where the lieutenants explained and monitored their duties. The first lieutenant in particular treated them as mere minions, and often sent them to deliver messages throughout the ship. Midshipmen performed service in the boats, particularly when the ship was in port, ferrying men and supplies between ship and shore. At sea they spent a considerable time amongst the men, whom they were expected to keep in order when working, especially aloft, or at general quarters, and to report to the lieutenants anyone thought work-shy or derelict in his duties. Like the lieutenants, midshipmen stood a watch at night, but their duties were not onerous, for in three watches they spent eight hours below for every four hours on deck.

Amongst their many duties, midshipmen ensured that hammocks were stowed each morning and cleaned regularly, and made a note of those sailors who lashed their hammocks improperly. They were barred from lounging against the guns or the sides of the ship, and were prohibited from walking the deck with their hands in their pockets. They were sometimes responsible for the working of the mizzen mast, or went aloft to furl the mizzen-royal and mizzen topgallant sail whenever sail was shortened. They were also expected to go aloft with the ordinary sailors to learn how to furl, reef, bend and unbend a sail, set up rigging and carry out all the other myriad tasks connected with seamanship. They could always be found in each top when sails were being furled in order to encourage and monitor the topmen (those performing tasks aloft) as they worked. Other duties of midshipmen included supervision of the hoisting in of stores, command of parties bringing in water, mustering the men at night and general tasks such as collecting and carrying for the lieutenants and captain. During watches at night they had to stay awake on the quarterdeck to help make soundings and mark a chalkboard with the ship's position, and be prepared to run errands for the officer of the watch.

Apart from a captain (the temporary rank of 'commodore' will be dealt with elsewhere) or admiral, the only other commissioned rank aboard a ship was lieutenant, a term derived from French – *lieu*, a place, and *tenir*, to hold – meaning that this officer served in the capacity of an absent captain or, less literally, simply placed him next in seniority where the captain was present. The number of lieutenants varied depending on the size of the ship. A first rate had eight, while a fifth rate had only three, with precedence determined by the dates of their commissions. The first lieutenant, responsible directly to the captain, ensured that the ship's functions were carried out properly and in a timely fashion, preserved discipline and ensured the proper navigation of the ship from one point to the next, according to the captain's orders. Junior lieutenants kept the watches, together with other tasks such as commanding sections of guns, managing administrative divisions, serving as signals officers, or as treasurers or caterers in the wardroom. All such tasks were set by the first lieutenant, who established the routine based on a combination of Admiralty regulations, the captain's wishes, his own views based on personal experience and naval tradition and precedent – what contemporaries sometimes termed 'the custom of the Service'. All such responsibilities fell to lieutenants aboard ships of the line – that is, ships where a captain filled the position of commanding officer – as well as aboard frigates.

A midshipman, by Cruikshank, showing the elaborate uniform of the 1790s that soon gave way to a more simplified outfit, including trousers and round or top hat. Midshipmen ranged greatly in age; not all of them fit the stereotyped image of boys or young teenagers. Certainly there were some under 14, but most were in their 20s, with a few in their 30s or even 40s – men who had failed to pass their exam for a lieutenancy. (Stratford Archive)

Royal Navy lieutenant, 1799, by Cruikshank. While the captain was generally responsible for the organization of the crew, the more detailed work, such as the allocation of all hands to watches and other tasks, fell to the first lieutenant. (Stratford Archive)

Much of a lieutenant's daily routine, like that of the ship's company in general, was mundane, such as the precautions he was to take to prevent accidents resulting from squalls or sudden shifts in the direction of the wind. He monitored the steering of the ship, seeing that a proper record of her position was entered into the logbook at regular intervals and that her course was maintained. For what little share of glamour and glory there was to be had by a lieutenant in the Royal Navy, there was – contrary to the claims of recruiting posters and sea-going uncles' yarns – much more in the way of routine and responsibility.

The first lieutenant functioned in effect as the captain's proxy, and consequently did most of the work. However, a lieutenant had a closer relationship with the men than did the captain, owing to the invisible barrier that permanently existed between a captain and his crew. Serving as he did fairly closely with the men beneath him, a newly appointed lieutenant naturally wished to establish a good rapport with the ship's company, doing his best to introduce himself in hopes of receiving a favourable reception.

As it was the captain's responsibility to see that the ship's company stood at full, or as close to full, strength, as possible, he periodically sent a lieutenant ashore with a party of 'press men' to undertake the unpleasant task of manning the ship, by force if necessary. To that end, some of the ship's boats would go ashore at nightfall, containing a lieutenant or master's mate in charge, and a group of sailors, to search the dockside brothels and sailors' taverns or simply to comb the streets for suitable quarry. Anyone who seemed fit enough for a seafaring life was dragged away, though occasionally members of his family or a sympathetic crowd would come to his rescue, not always successfully. Press gangs did not carry firearms or edged weapons on such excursions, apart from the occasional cutlass, and even then they were wielded more to intimidate than to cause harm. Clubs and belaying pins were, however, resorted to when necessary. Watermen and merchantmen were particularly sought after, as well as dockside labourers. In short, press gangs specifically sought those connected with the sea, but so great was the need for men, particularly for a ship of the line, that landsmen were considered acceptable prey. While they possessed no maritime skills, they could help man the guns and carry out unskilled tasks, at least until they acquired some knowledge of the ship and its functions. Once aboard these men were held below, guarded by a Marine sentry. The practice of impressment was by no means confined to men on land. Homeward-bound merchantmen, especially those nearing port, were sometimes boarded to see what they could offer.

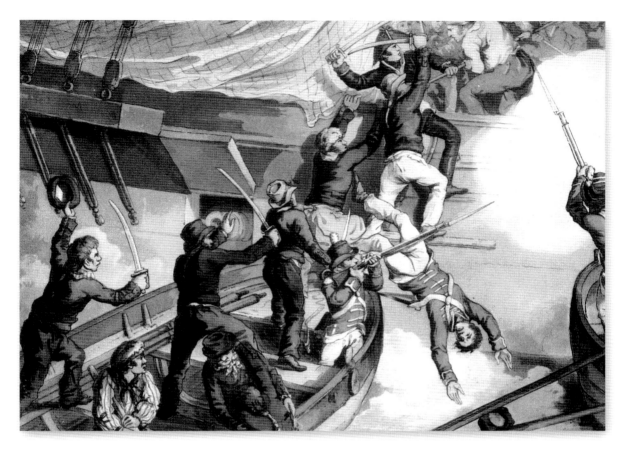

Boarding action led by a lieutenant of HMS *Surprise*, retaking HMS *Hermione* off Puerto Cabello, Venezuela, in October 1799, two years after the crew had mutinied and handed the ship over to the Spanish. (Stratford Archive)

At sea the first lieutenant stood no watch at night, but was expected to be on duty on the decks throughout the course of the day and to come up during night watches when danger threatened or problems required his presence. A lieutenant of the watch had to see that the helmsmen kept the ship on course, that the log was updated every hour, and that the rate of sailing was marked on the board that stood on the quarterdeck. The men had to be monitored to see that they were alert and properly turned out, at their correct stations, and ready to carry out the next order, whenever that might be issued. Further, according to Falconer: 'The first lieutenant is to prevent all profane swearing and abusive language; all disturbance, noise, and confusion; to enforce a strict obedience to orders, a proper respect to all superiors, and an observance of discipline and good order; and he is to report to the captain all those whose misconduct he shall think deserving of reprehension or punishment.'

The lieutenant had to ensure that the midshipmen and master's mates performed their duties. He had to muster the watch, keep the ship in her station within the squadron or fleet, and to report the sighting of unidentified ships and shifts of wind. He had to make sure that the lookout men at the mastheads and elsewhere were awake and did not remain too long at their stations. When the captain was in his quarters in the evening and an unidentified ship (known to contemporaries as a 'strange sail') was sighted, he sent a midshipman to inform the captain. While the captain got dressed to come to the quarterdeck, the lieutenant got the ship ready for action, keeping the vessel beyond gunshot until the captain and crew were ready. During the night, he was to be particularly attentive in seeing that the master-at-arms and corporals made their appointed half-hourly rounds of all sections of the ship to see that no trouble existed amongst the men, that no candles or lamps were burning (apart from those specifically allowed), that no one was smoking, except in the galley, and that sentinels stood at their appointed positions. Further, as Falconer observed, 'The lieutenant who commands the watch at sea, keeps a list of all the officers and men thereto belonging, in order to muster them when he judges it expedient, and report to the captain the names of those who are absent from their duty.'

A lieutenant had to ensure that the men kept themselves clean, that the hammocks were washed and the men's clothes scrubbed. The task of inspecting the ship's firearms fell to the junior lieutenants, who also led the men in musketry practice, for at some point sailors might be required to fight on shore. If the captain were ashore, virtually all the powers of this omnipotent officer passed into the hands of the first lieutenant. Thus, he could place another officer under arrest, or have him put in irons, though he was not authorized to release or otherwise punish any transgressor unless the captain were absent for an extended period. It was also the lieutenant's responsibility to prevent any boats from coming alongside or leaving the ship without his specific instructions.

A lieutenant sent one of the carpenter's mates to sound the ship's well on two occasions during each watch, and to see that the lower gun deck ports were properly closed. Each morning a lieutenant had to receive reports on the state of the rigging from the boatswain, and from the carpenter respecting the state of the masts and yards. Where problems connected with these features were discovered, a report was issued to the captain. A lieutenant also had to monitor the admiral's signals, to answer them as soon as his signalman reported them, and to record them accurately in the ship's log. During the night, he ensured that the lanterns were lit, and that all the guns were loaded, should the need arise to fire a signal. He was also responsible for seeing that the cabin windows and ports were closed to ensure that the ship's lights could not be seen from a distance. In foggy conditions he ordered fog signals, which could

E **BOAT ACTION**

A lieutenant (**1**) leads a party of sailors (**2**) and a Marine (**3**) in a boat action against an American vessel during the war of 1812–15. Quite apart from glory and the prospect of promotion, the lure of prize money was easy to appreciate, for at the start of the war with France in 1793 pay in the Royal Navy had not been increased in generations, though this would gradually change. Officers, earning a disproportionate share of prize money, naturally felt inclined to capture enemy vessels both to supplement their pay and to enhance their reputations. Boat actions, like this one, moreover ensured that the captors took the prize intact, rather than pounding it into submission by gunfire, and therefore presented an object of greater value to an Admiralty Prize Court, which on the North American station was at Halifax. On the termination of an extended and successful cruise officers sometimes received considerable sums – including those senior officers who, though not directly involved in a capture, nevertheless commanded the squadron responsible for taking the spoils, whether merchant or naval.

Up to 1808 the proportion of prize money allotted to officers comprised: flag officer, one-eighth, captain, two-eighths and lieutenants, one-eighth. This left one-eighth for warrant officers, one-eighth for petty officers, and two-eighths for the remainder of the crew, including Marines. After 1808, the system was altered, thus: captain, two-eighths, of which the flag officer shared one-third; the share for lieutenants and warrant officers remained unchanged; while petty officers, the remainder of the crew, and Marines received four-eighths.

Notwithstanding the ferocity of action depicted here, exposure to enemy fire and the parry and thrust of sword and cutlass in fact accounted for far fewer injuries and fatalities than accidents and disease. Midshipman Lord Henry Lennox, the 14-year-old fourth son of the Duke of Richmond, for instance, fell to his death after slipping on a yard while furling sail aboard the *Blake* in 1812. For those who performed no such tasks, disease did not discriminate between ranks, while wrecks were the largest single cause of ship losses. An officer like this young lieutenant had not only to keep his wits about him to ensure proper navigation, but also to be vigilant against fire and explosion. In short, combat numbered among a series of threats to his life at sea. Note that, during this period, the American flag consisted of 15 stripes and 15 stars.

Captain (later Admiral) Sir Sidney Smith. Vainglorious, egotistical, yet excessively brave and patriotic, Smith, like Nelson, Cochrane and many other distinguished Royal Navy officers of the time, revelled in surmounting impossible odds and performing feats of derring-do, earning for himself a heroic, if flawed, reputation. (Author's collection)

consist of beating a drum, striking the ship's bell, firing some of the guns, or a combination of these. He was required to maintain a logbook, according to the form specified by the Admiralty, which he signed and submitted to the Navy Board before receiving his pay. He was also responsible, when called upon by the captain, to draft reports for the Admiralty that the captain would then sign and pass on.

Captains

The captain was all powerful aboard his ship. He was not only its commander, but the judge of all transgressors. His word was absolute and seldom did he alter a sentence once rendered. His power over the crew extended almost over life itself. As discussed earlier, he could not order the death sentence without convening a court martial attended by his equals, but he could order a flogging severe enough to bring a man close to death, and some actually did succumb under the lash as a result of blood loss and shock. He also possessed the power to demote and promote his officers, and to send men to the brig. In the modern era such power, short of a sovereign, has perhaps never been exercised over one's subordinates as that of a captain during the Napoleonic Wars. Put simply, the captain was responsible for absolutely everything and everyone aboard his ship; he was the highest authority and his word was law. Naturally, captains varied greatly in terms of character and practice, and expressed their authority in an individual manner: some were austere and detached, others cheerful and approachable. Some took a stern line with respect to discipline and thus ruled by the lash, while others were relatively benign and sought to command through courage and personal example.

Once a captain received appointment to a ship he made his way, commission from the Admiralty in hand, to wherever she might lay in port. Once aboard, he received from the master-attendant of the dockyard a new narrow pennant, a red-and-white piece of bunting fashioned in a swallow tail,

Evacuation of a ship on fire. Captains faced numerous potential hazards, including leaks, running aground in darkness, the loss of masts through rigging failure or from improper handling during a squall, and, worst of all, fire. The loss of a ship always resulted in an official inquiry, followed by a court martial. (Author's collection)

which was hoisted to the masthead. When the captain came aboard – and indeed whenever he appeared on deck thereafter – the lieutenants immediately moved to the lee side of the deck, out of respect. No one addressed him except with a matter relating to the duties of the day, and no sailor spoke to the captain without first removing his hat. Upon his return to the ship from a visit ashore, the officers and crew assembled in his honour, standing at attention as he approached. The boatswain stood at the gangway to 'pipe the side', that is, blowing a solemn salute with his whistle, as the captain reached the deck. Marine sentries stood to attention and the officers, midshipmen and men all fell in. All was silent, apart from the sound of the boatswain's whistle. As he stepped aboard, the captain saluted those assembled on the quarterdeck and walked to his cabin. When he left the ship, all hands assembled in like manner.

On first appearing before his assembled officers and crew, the captain read his commission, or 'read himself in'. First impressions were important as, after all, the ship's company were in all probability destined to share their lives (and in some cases deaths) together in close proximity, perhaps for many years to come. The captain therefore acquainted himself with the officers and crew before setting about fitting her for sea. Some captains sought to institute changes, which were sometimes resented, for they represented a departure from the usual routine to which the crew had become accustomed under their previous captain. Seaman William Robinson's new captain was, for instance, instantly loathed for ordering his men to paint over the chequered design which Nelson had ordered adorned on all the ships in his fleet just prior to Trafalgar. Nothing was better calculated to alienate a ship's company than to tamper with so obvious a mark of distinguished service. That said, all such changes fell squarely within the captain's remit, and occasionally alterations were made for the better, reforming the bad practices of his predecessor and introducing improved forms of seamanship.

Nelson in a boat action off Cadiz, July 1797, on the southern coast of Spain, where his coxswain, John Sykes, twice saved his life. As William Robinson, a veteran of Trafalgar would later write, 'a seaman will as soon risk his life for his kind and good captain, as he would to defend his country's honour'. (Author's collection)

Captain leading divine service, a responsibility he performed every Sunday unless he had a chaplain aboard. He also conducted funerals on deck that invariably concluded with a burial at sea. (National Maritime Museum)

Apart from exercising the discretionary power to alter the ship's routine, every captain had to examine all the guns, gun carriages, muskets, cutlasses and other small arms, and reject or have repaired any defective weapons. He kept inventories of all stores sent on board and the counterparts issued to him by his warrant officers, such as those of the boatswain and gunner. He also kept an account of the ship's provisions, indicating the daily expenditure of food, drink, ammunition and other stores, all of which inventories and records he had regularly to report to the Admiralty, partly for the sake of ensuring resupply, and partly with an eye to the prevention of fraud and pilfering.

Above all, he had to man his ship, for unless he was assuming command of a vessel already in commission, there was no crew waiting for him. In short, if the ship were newly placed in commission after construction, or was being returned to service after decommissioning, then the captain's first task was to fill its complement. Unlike today, the Navy took no responsibility for supplying a newly commissioned vessel with a crew, apart from the handful of men who

 CAPTAIN'S CABIN

Accommodation for commissioned officers (called simply 'commission' officers at the time) varied according to the size of the ship, but was generally located in the same place in ships of the line and frigates. For both admirals and captains, his large cabin was usually subdivided by canvas screens into a suite of rooms, with a day cabin, a sleeping cabin, and an area for dining. From here he could walk to two quarter galleries, one of which served as his private toilet and the other as a sort of office and observation post from which to watch the handling of the sails. Access to the captain's area was only possible through one entrance, over which a Royal Marine sentry stood guard around the clock. Within the confined space of their cabins captains had to share space with guns. When the crews were called to action, the cabin partitions were removed and the officers' personal possessions stowed away so that the gunners could operate their weapons without hindrance. Partitions were generally made only of canvas, sometimes mounted on a wooden frame, but the captain's quarters could be separated off entirely by wooden panels. To assist him, the captain had a small retinue of servants, varying in number according to the size of the ship.

remained constantly aboard to maintain a ship that sat 'in ordinary'. According to contemporary practice, all hands were entered on to the ship's books directly and were thus not officially employed by the Navy, but rather belonged to the ship and, thus, her captain. The captain obtained men principally from two sources, the first of which, as discussed earlier, consisted of the insidious method of impressment. The second depended on the uncertain number of volunteers who chose to enlist for service aboard a particular vessel, usually in response to various methods of inducement dangled before them: placards posted in cities large and small – but especially in seaside towns – promising rapid promotion, large amounts of prize money, free rations, adventure and other enticements to all who would join the ship's company. The captain also established a rendezvous at a sailors' tavern where the master-at-arms and coxswain could persuade would-be tars to join the crew. As well as an established rate of pay, the captain would offer a bounty or one-off payment to those who signed up. Many of those impressed accepted their fate and offered to 'volunteer', thus securing for themselves the King's bounty, but rendering it impossible to determine, statistically, exactly what proportion of a crew had joined by their own volition. The captain had to content himself with all manner of other malcontents, such as those given the choice between hanging or service at sea, fugitives from the law, debt, a bad marriage or other difficult circumstances. Some were sent by the Lord Mayor of London, having been found drunk in the streets. In all, perhaps a third of a ship's company was composed of landsmen and an eighth were foreigners.

At some point the captain examined both volunteers and impressed men for purposes of determining their fitness for service at sea. The surgeon examined them too to ensure that they were not infested or infected. Those found too ill or weak to work were discharged. A man who was merely dirty could be washed and his clothes fumigated. Once he had assembled sufficient numbers of men, the captain had each man's name entered in the ship's books, particularly the muster book, in which, in order to identify deserters, a record was kept of the man's physical features, including hair and eye colour, chest size and any tattoos that adorned his body. If a man deserted, details of the circumstances and the sailor concerned were sent to the Admiralty. The captain sent his muster books every month or two to the Lords Commissioners of the Admiralty, which examined them for such things as deductions made to the pay of members of the crew. In all cases, the captain was expected to vouch for the accuracy of all such records, not least so that he could not draw the pay of seamen who had been discharged – indicated in the muster book by the initial 'D', or 'DD' for 'Discharged Dead', or 'R', for 'Run', the Navy's term for desertion.

At sea the captain was responsible for the ship, and for the whole of the ship's company. In short, he bore a great responsibility, as Falconer explains: 'The charge of a captain in his Majesty's navy is very comprehensive, inasmuch as he is not only answerable for any bad conduct in the military government, navigation, and equipment of the ship he commands; but also for any neglect of duty, or ill management in his inferior officers, whose several charges he is appointed to superintend and regulate.' His responsibilities varied greatly: he ensured that the lieutenant made out his quarter bills which stated the tasks and stations of all hands; he kept the keys to the magazines and saw that they were protected against unauthorized entry. He had to remain alert to the possibility of fire by forbidding the use of candles in certain parts of the ship and while alcohol was being removed from the spirit room. He ordered all lights out at

8pm each night and forbade smoking in all parts of the ship except the galley, where of course fire already existed in the stove. He had to ensure that the men received sufficient training at gunnery and at small-arms fire, and that the colours were not kept flying in stormy weather. He was required to keep a journal and log in duplicate, for the sake of the Admiralty, and at the end of a cruise had to send an account of the state of the ship to the Lords Commissioners.

The captain was in charge of certain supplies known as 'slops', mostly in the form of bedding and clothing, which he sold to those members of the crew who required them, often via the ship's purser. He was required to keep his ship clean, dry and well ventilated by having the men sweep and scrub the decks, open the ports, pump the wells and bilges, and ensure the proper functioning of the windsails (or ventilators), which were fitted to expel foul air from the hold. The captain had to punish wrongdoers, discourage vice and immorality, uphold – as he interpreted it – his country's honour, protect the secrecy of the signals and signal book and, above all, 'burn, sink and destroy' as many enemy vessels as possible. He was expected to display unimpeachable personal conduct, being, Falconer stipulated, 'enjoined to shew [sic] a laudable example of honour and virtue to the officers and men, and to discountenance all dissolute, immoral, and disorderly practices, and such as are contrary to the rules of discipline and subordination, as well as to correct those who are guilty of such offences as are punishable according to the usage of the sea.' Unlike

Sir Sidney Smith standing on the walls of the fortified city of Acre on the coast of Palestine, May 1799. Although only the captain of HMS *Tigre*, Smith unilaterally assumed the rank of commodore and organized the Turkish defence of the city against the French under Bonaparte. Simultaneously, he was serving with authority from the Foreign Office as joint minister to Turkey, which in turn had granted him temporary command of its army and navy in the Levant. Such were the various roles naval officers could play on active service. (Author's collection)

Admiral Lord Nelson, who enjoyed a degree of popularity across the Navy that remains unmatched to this day. (Author's collection)

practically everyone else on board, the captain stood no watch and did not intervene in the ordinary working of the ship unless a problem arose. He was also obliged to keep the crew acquainted with his own rules and the practices he intended to see observed aboard his vessel, in addition to Admiralty regulations – the Articles of War discussed earlier. The fact that captains fairly regularly ordered a flogging did not, in the eyes of his crew, make him either a martinet or a sadist. In an age in which whole swathes of British society suffered from widespread poverty, deprivation, disease, premature death and long prison sentences or even capital punishment for a range of infractions that today's society scarcely recognizes as justifying incarceration, the crew accepted the captain's need to use the lash to keep a tight ship – so long as he did not abuse his power.

In fact, notwithstanding the Spartan or even harsh conditions of shipboard life, some captains enjoyed immense popularity, commanding respect and even love, for they recognized that the best of a man was drawn out by engendering his respect rather than propagating fear. Some ships' companies banded together to pay for the purchase of silver plates to be presented as keepsakes to captains upon the conclusion of a cruise, but in most cases the captain kept his distance from the crew and maintained tight discipline at all times, for captains considered too soft or lenient were not respected. Each one maintained his own ideas about seamanship and to a certain extent his own routine. He was free to exercise his own whims and to enforce them on the crew, whether it be in the dress of the men, the leave he permitted or the entertainments tolerated. Most, for instance, would allow women aboard when the ship lay in port, for it was understood that while seamen, for fear of desertion, should be denied shore leave, it was only reasonable to allow them access to women, whether they be wives or women of dubious character. Others adamantly believed the practice encouraged licentiousness. Admiralty regulations specifically barred captains from themselves having women aboard – apart from official visits conducted by the wives of superior officers – and they could face a court martial for any infraction of this regulation. The logic of this was plain for all to appreciate: with shore leave a captain's right, there could be no justification for his entertaining a female visitor aboard a vessel of war.

In addition to carrying out his functions at sea, captains were occasionally entrusted with duties otherwise performed by diplomats and consuls under the auspices of the Foreign Office. When, for instance, Britain had no consular representation at Algiers, it dispatched Captain Lord Cochrane to demand the release of a captured British vessel taken in retaliation for an Algerian vessel seized while violating the law of blockade.

Admirals

There were four types of admiral, in descending order of rank: admiral of the fleet, of which there was only one – and generally a ceremonial and not a seagoing post – (full) admiral, vice admiral and rear admiral. A full admiral was the most senior officer in command of a fleet, with a union flag flown at the main topgallant masthead. A vice admiral, who also often commanded a fleet, was distinguished by a flag displayed at the fore topgallant masthead. A rear admiral, who usually commanded a squadron, carried his flag at the mizzen topgallant masthead. There were always far more admirals, of all types, than fleets or squadrons for them to command, on account of the fact that promotion was normally by seniority; thus, so long as an officer remained in the Navy, he was likely eventually to reach the rank of admiral, even if he had long since ceased to serve at sea. In 1812, for instance, the Royal Navy had, apart from the admiral of the fleet, 21 admirals of the red squadron, 20 admirals of the white, 20 admirals of the blue, 22 vice admirals of the red, 19 vice admirals of the red, 17 rear admirals of the white, and 24 rear admirals of the blue, together with 31 rear admirals who never hoisted their flag, but were superannuated on half pay.

Admiral Edward Pellew, first Viscount Exmouth (1757–1833). One of the most outstanding frigate captains of the era, he is also remembered for the successful bombardment of Algiers in 1816, which led to the release of hundreds of European slaves. Exmouth expected high standards from his officers and men, from whom he received their respect, though not perhaps their love. (Author's collection)

Further explanation of this arcane and somewhat confusing hierarchy may be instructive. Each fleet was subdivided into squadrons that theoretically meant that, following a system of seniority, the admiral's squadron flew a red flag, the vice admiral's squadron a white flag, and the rear admiral's squadron a blue flag. However, by the time of the French Revolutionary and Napoleonic Wars, fleets had grown so large that it was impossible for a single admiral to exercise proper control of his squadron's movements from his position in the centre of the fleet. The Navy therefore sought to allocate three admirals to a squadron, with a full admiral in command, a vice admiral as his second-in-command, and a rear admiral as his third-in-command. In theory, the white squadron was commanded by an admiral of the white, with subordinates in the form of a vice admiral of the white and a rear admiral of the white. Promotion for admirals also took place in this manner, with the elevation of a rear admiral of the blue – the lowest position on the ladder of promotion within flag rank – to rear admiral of the white, and a rear admiral of the red becoming a vice admiral of the blue, and so on up to admiral of the fleet. Stated simply, between 1805 and 1815 the ladder of promotion stood as follows, in descending order: admiral of the fleet; admiral of the red; admiral of the white; admiral of the blue; vice admiral of the red; vice admiral of the white; vice admiral of the blue; rear admiral of the red; rear admiral of the white; rear admiral of the blue.

Upon assuming command, whether of a fleet of 20 ships or more, or merely of a squadron of ten or 12, the admiral sent notification to all the captains on his station. He then made his way to his home port, perhaps Portsmouth or Chatham, there to hoist his pennant and establish himself in his quarters. In all likelihood he would find on his desk dispatches sent by his subordinate admirals or captains, announcing their arrival on station and any subsequent communications, since naturally an admiral expected regular reports from his juniors. Once at his station – an expanse of water for which he was responsible – an admiral issued orders to squadron commanders within the fleet, or to individual ship captains if local strength only amounted to a single squadron. On occasion he would have instructions for a group of ships serving within a particular squadron, or those cruising on detached duty.

Whatever his station and the nature of his task, an admiral had to possess certain qualities, some of which Falconer described thus:

> His skill should [enable him] to counteract the various disasters which his squadron may suffer from different causes. His vigilance and presence of mind are necessary to seize every favourable

Nelson mortally wounded on the quarterdeck of the *Victory*. While the decorations on his coat rendered him particularly conspicuous to enemy marksmen, officers' bicornes and epaulettes alone sufficed to identify them as prime targets. (Author's collection)

opportunity that his situation may offer, to prosecute his principal design; to extricate himself from any difficulty or distress; to check unfortunate events in the beginning, and retard the progress of any great calamity. He should be endued with resolution, and fortitude to animate his officers by the force of

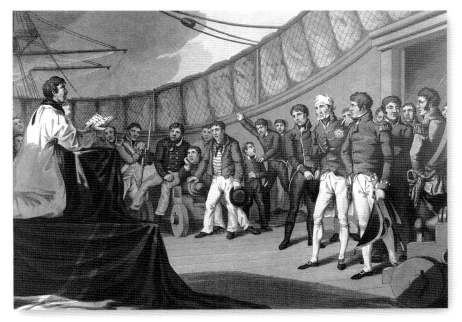

Nelson, straddled by lieutenants from the *Vanguard*, together with ordinary seamen, attends church service after the battle of the Nile in August 1798. (Royal Naval Museum)

Admiral Alexander Hood, Viscount Bridport (1726–1814). The younger brother of Samuel (later Admiral Viscount) Hood, his service during the French Revolutionary and Napoleonic Wars is most associated with the Quiberon Expedition of 1795, the mutiny at Spithead and the blockade of Brest. (Author's collection)

example, and promote a sense of emulation in those who are under his command, as well to improve any advantage, as to frustrate or defeat the efforts of his enemies.

Those accounted for but a few of the many skills required of an admiral, whose competent knowledge of the seas, weather and winds, and of the coast or area in which he was stationed, was paramount. With this knowledge, he could establish an advantage over his enemy, enabling him to attack on the most favourable occasion or prepare for his own defence. If his squadron was forced by rough seas or stormy weather to shelter in a bay or road, an admiral needed to maintain enough frigates at sea to provide him with intelligence respecting his opponent's position and probable intentions, so that he could weigh anchor and take appropriate action once weather permitted pursuit. An admiral also had to form his ships in line ahead for the sake of his subordinate officers, who could thereby practise this manoeuvre, keep to their appointed stations and maintain this formation when they tacked, veered or sailed abreast. An admiral had to be able to form his fleet or squadron into a proper order of battle,

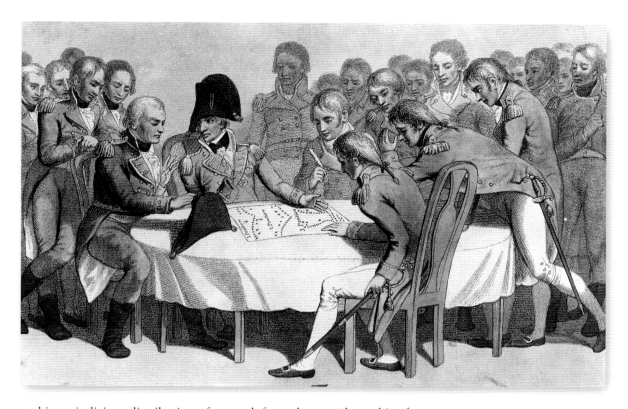

making a judicious distribution of strength from the van (those ships foremost in the line) to the rear, deploying the principal force in the centre, in order to defend himself from the enemy, who might otherwise break through the line and leave the van and rear unsupported.

Yet an admiral required more than the mere technical skills – impressive though these may be – required to manoeuvre a squadron or fleet across vast stretches of water. Maximum fighting efficiency was only possible by maintaining a strong professional relationship with one's captains, even if actual friendship did not always figure prominently. Still, in some cases, a genuine filial bond developed, most notably between Nelson and his captains – what he called his 'Band of Brothers' – during the Nile campaign of 1798, which continued until his death seven years later. George Duff's description to his wife of the affection felt by those serving under Nelson numbered amongst many expressed by captains who were prepared to serve their admiral with implicit confidence: 'He is so good and pleasant a man that we all wish to do what he likes, without any kind of orders. I have been myself very lucky with most of my Admirals; but I really think the present the pleasantest I have met with …'. Nor were such views confined to those holding a commission. William Robinson, an ordinary seaman, reflected the general opinion of the lower ranks when he wrote how Nelson 'was adored, and in fighting under him, every man thought himself sure of success …'. Similarly, Henry Walker, a midshipman in the *Bellerophon*, echoed the sentiments of many in Nelson's fleet at Trafalgar when he identified the admiral's presence as all that was required to generate an atmosphere of invincibility: 'Though we had before no doubt of success in the event of an action, yet the presence of such a man could not but inspire every individual in the fleet with additional confidence. Every one felt himself more than a match for the enemy.'

Vice Admiral Lord Nelson, surrounded by his captains on the eve of Trafalgar, explains his plan of attack, which he described to Lady Hamilton as not only 'generally approved, but clearly perceived and understood'. (Royal Naval Museum)

An admiral was also to be sufficiently acquainted with naval law to be able to conduct himself properly in a court martial. Some knowledge of foreign languages, or at least those of the countries with whom Britain was at war, especially French, was useful, so that he could interpret documents seized from the enemy and thus ascertain his plans and intentions. An admiral was also expected to have a good working knowledge of geometry so as to be able to conduct surveys of uncharted coasts, roads or harbours, as well as to revise existing maps and to correct navigational errors based on any new information he acquired through hydrography. He was expected to be able to determine latitude and longitude wherever he was, and had to be sufficiently knowledgeable of astronomy and lunar observation to be able to navigate his own ship properly, and also convey orders to the numerous ships constituting the squadron or squadrons under his command.

According to his instructions from the Navy Board, he was to assist in all councils of war that related to naval affairs and to visit, as often as possible, the other ships in his squadron, examining their condition and making enquiries amongst his captains as to the state of their respective crews, provisions and vessels, and the clarity with which they understood both their duties and instructions. The admiral was to inspect the men mustered, ensuring that every sailor was rated and stationed according to his abilities, at the same time making sure that no 'supernumeraries' were listed in the ship's books, which of course entailed unnecessary expense. All of this business, and much more besides, an admiral was required to report to the Secretary of the Admiralty, who then conveyed this information to the Lords Commissioners. On his return to Britain, he was personally to report to his superiors in London with a written account of his voyage or expedition and a copy of his journal for inspection.

When battle appeared imminent, an admiral acquainted his second-in-command with what was expected of him and issued general orders to his fleet, as Nelson did in October 1805 on the eve of Trafalgar, distilling his thoughts into simple written instructions, on the basis that in the smoke and confusion of battle individual ship captains might not be able to see signals hoisted aboard the flagship or those communicated in turn by the frigates: 'The Second in Command will in all possible things direct the movements of his Line, by keeping them as compact as the nature of circumstances will admit. Captains are to look to their particular Line, as their rallying point. But in case Signals cannot be either seen or perfectly understood, no Captain can do very wrong, if he places his Ship alongside that of an Enemy.' Such instructions highlight a fact well appreciated in the age of sail, but perhaps less so in today's era of instantaneous communication: command of a squadron or fleet was a sufficiently complex affair as to oblige even the most experienced admiral often to make decisions without recourse to advice from fellow officers; and, having issued his instructions, to leave their interpretation to the discretion of his subordinates as circumstances changed, without further clarification. The same principles governed an admiral's relationship with London, where orders were necessarily drafted in general terms to enable an admiral to make judgements based on changing circumstances, with aid or advice weeks if not months away. Not only had an admiral limited contact with the Admiralty, he relied heavily on local intelligence via his frigates, which were known to contemporaries as the 'eyes of the fleet'. So crucial to his operations were his frigates that admirals regularly complained of their dearth.

Extended service exacted a heavy price on the health of admirals, particularly those on active stations such as the Channel and the Mediterranean, but above all on those, irrespective of their particular post, serving on blockade duty. This was an exceedingly arduous and trying business, with month upon tedious month spent lying off a foreign port monitoring a hostile squadron or fleet, with little to relieve the intense boredom except the distant hope that the enemy would emerge and provoke battle. Those whose responsibilities lay chiefly in cruising great distances also bore the scars of interminable months or years of service, with the toll exacted sometimes forcing admirals to premature retirement. A worse fate befell a handful of others, most notably Vice Admiral Cuthbert Collingwood, Nelson's successor in the Mediterranean, who literally worked himself to death through constant service at sea. As early as September 1805, he complained of his lot to his father-in-law, yet refused to take leave during the whole of the period between that time and his death in 1810, notwithstanding the relative quiet of his station after Trafalgar.

EXPERIENCE OF BATTLE AND AFTERMATH

In action, midshipmen supervised the sailors' work with the rigging and sails, and at the guns, or where required took up the fighting themselves as marksmen or as part of a boarding party, with dirk, pistol or musket in hand. For lieutenants, the most important function was preparing the ship for action,

Admiralty Board Room, 1808. As most of the men around the table held an admiral's rank, they could bring years of experience to the task of formulating naval strategy, not to mention their myriad other responsibilities. (Stratford Archive)

and thereafter to supervise those doing the fighting. Thirty-four-year-old Lieutenant William Cumby of the *Bellerophon* summarized the morning of Trafalgar when he went 'round the decks to see everything in its place and all in perfect order, before I reported to the Captain the ship in readiness for action …', noting how 'the zeal of the seamen had led them to chalk in large characters on their guns the words, "Victory or Death" – a very gratifying mark of the spirit with which they were going to their work'. Once action commenced, a lieutenant watched to see that no loose powder lay on the deck and, if in command of a battery of guns, ensured that the gun captains discharged their weapons only after sighting them to the best advantage. Above all, he was responsible for seeing that the men both remained at their stations and served the guns with all the energy they could muster. Lieutenants also commanded small groups of sailors in boat actions, led boarding parties and commanded landing parties that undertook raids against naval installations or enemy ships anchored in port.

 ACTION ON THE LOWER GUN DECK OF A SHIP OF THE LINE
In this typical scene in the midst of battle, a lieutenant (**1**) and midshipman (**2**) shout instructions to a gun crew while they prime the charge and manhandle a 24-pdr into position before firing. Notwithstanding the risks, in a macabre sort of way midshipmen looked forward to battle, for losses amongst their officers necessarily translated themselves into opportunities for promotion, a circumstance illustrated by Dr Beatty who, aboard the *Victory* at Trafalgar, recalled how Nelson, while standing on the poop deck with a wry smile on his face, addressed a group of midshipmen thus: 'This day or to-morrow will be a fortunate one for you, young men.'

Sailors and Marines fight their way aboard an enemy vessel in a boat action under the command of a midshipman, depicted here in his distinctive uniform, pike in hand. (Angus Konstam)

Captains played a rather different role in action. The moment a lookout perceived the presence of a strange vessel the captain was summoned on deck, where he immediately issued signals to his admiral (provided, of course, he was not serving independently) and, if necessary, called the ship's company to their respective stations, or 'beat to quarters'. At 6am on the morning of Trafalgar, Midshipman Badcock in the *Neptune* observed this standard routine:

The sun rose, which, as it ascended from its bed of ocean, looked hazy and watery, as if it smiled in tears on many brave hearts which fate had decreed would never see it set. It was my morning watch; I was midshipman on the forecastle, and at the first dawn of day a forest of strange masts was seen to leeward. I ran aft and informed the officer of the watch. The captain was on deck in a moment, and ere it was well light, the signals were flying through the fleet to bear up and form the order of sailing in two columns.

With the bulkheads removed from his cabin and all other partitions down the entire length of the ship stowed in the hold – thus creating an unimpeded gun deck – the captain would issue general orders and might devote some time to write to his wife before conducting a tour of the ship, offering encouraging words and appealing to the men's patriotism as he went. Just prior to Trafalgar, Captain Charles Mansfield, in command of the *Minotaur*, summoned the crew's courage thus:

> Men, we are now in sight of the enemy whom there is every probability of engaging, and I trust that this day will prove the most glorious our country ever saw. I shall say nothing to you of courage. Our country never produced a coward. For my own part I pledge myself to the officers and ship's company not to quit the ship I may get alongside of till either she strikes [i.e. surrenders] or sinks – or I sink.
>
> I have only to recommend silence, and a strict attention to the orders of your officers. Be careful to take good aim, for it is to no purpose to throw shot away. You will now, every man, repair to your respective stations, and depend [on it], I will bring the ship into action as soon as possible. God save the King!

Volunteer Able Seaman John Cash, serving aboard the *Tonnant*, related a similar scene: 'Our good captain called all hands and said, "My lads, this will be a glorious day for us and the groundwork of a speedy return to our home[s]." He then ordered bread and cheese, and butter and beer for every man at the guns. I was one of them, and, believe me, we ate and drank, and

Nelson leading a boarding party onto the deck of the *San Josef* during the battle of St Vincent, 14 February 1797, when he held the rank of commodore. Note the lieutenant in cocked hat behind him. (Umhey Collection)

Captain Philip Broke (centre left) of HMS *Shannon*, capturing the American frigate *Chesapeake* in zune 1813. In such boarding actions captains shared the same risks as their men. (Stratford Archive)

were as cheerful as ever we had been over a pot of beer.' Midshipman Henry Walker in the *Bellerophon* described the same practice, by his own captain, John Cooke, who '… went below and exhorted his men on every deck, most earnestly entreating them to remember the words of their gallant Admiral [Nelson] just communicated by signal [i.e. 'England expects that every man will do his duty]. … He was cheered on his return upward [to the quarterdeck] by the whole ship's company who wrote on their guns in chalk: *Bellerophon*! Death or Glory!'

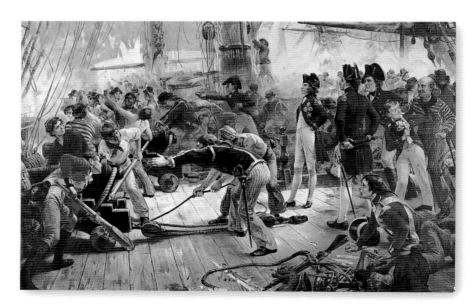

A gun crew in action, with Nelson and senior officers looking on. (Royal Naval Museum)

Nelson on the quarterdeck of the *San Josef* at the battle of St Vincent, 14 February 1797, accepting the sword of surrender from the mortally wounded Spanish captain. (Author's collection)

Sometimes, in conjunction with such exhortations, the captain issued general instructions in the course of his tour of the ship, as Robinson recalled at Trafalgar: '… our captain had given orders not to fire until we got close in with them, so that all our shots might tell; indeed, these were his words: "We shall want all our shot when we get close in: never mind their firing: when I fire a carronade from the quarter-deck, that will be a signal for you to begin, and I know you will do your duty as Englishmen."' Having carried out this essential duty, the captain assumed his place on the quarterdeck, there to await signals from the admiral (unless his vessel were operating singly), to ensure that his vessel manoeuvred accordingly – sailing either in line of battle or on an individual course as befitted his instructions – to send messages below and to receive regular reports concerning damage to the ship and casualties sustained. According to Falconer, the captain, having taken up his position on the quarterdeck, was expected '… to take all opportunities of annoying his enemy, and improving every advantage over him; to exhibit an example of courage and fortitude to his officers and crew; and to place his ship opposite to his adversary, in such a position, as that every cannon shall do effectual execution'.

Despite the absence of formal rules of war, a number of well-known conventions were generally observed by both sides, including those concerning a captain's decision to surrender his ship, which entitled him to haul down his colours with honour if it was believed he had done all that could reasonably be expected by way of resistance, and providing his casualties and damage were sufficient to render defeat inevitable. The same applied if an enemy boarding party 'carried' the ship. To signify surrender the captain would order the national flag hauled down, which explains why ships carried so many ensigns – to prevent misunderstanding if in battle one were shot away. A vanquished captain offered his sword, if possible with some degree of solemnity, to the senior officer of the opposing vessel, who, in an age where some vestiges of chivalry remained, sometimes returned it.

Lord Nelson as he lay dying on the starboard side of the cockpit of the *Victory*, 21 October 1805, his hand held by the ship's surgeon, William Beatty. Captain Thomas Hardy stands behind the admiral, while several midshipmen may be seen at right. (Author's collection)

In battle an admiral stood on the quarterdeck of his flagship, exposed to the same dangers as every other man above decks, a fact highlighted by Nelson's death at Trafalgar. Even before falling mortally wounded he had come close to injury, as had Captain Hardy, as witnessed by William Beatty, the surgeon aboard the *Victory*: '... a shot struck the brace bits on the quarter deck, and passed between Lord Nelson and Captain Hardy; a splinter from the bits bruising Captain Hardy's foot, and tearing the buckle from his shoe'. Nelson was not animated by the fact, for the simple reason that admirals appreciated that their subordinates looked to them for guidance, example and inspiration; in short, composure maintained under fire was absolutely vital if fighting efficiency and morale were to be maintained or even enhanced. Collingwood's composure prior to Trafalgar as described by William Smith, the admiral's 21-year-old servant, was not untypical of the behaviour displayed by senior officers of the Royal Navy in the age of fighting sail: '[I] ... entered the Admiral's cabin about daylight, and found him up and already dressing. He asked me if I had seen the French fleet; and on my replying that I had not, he told me to look at them. I then observed a crowd of ships to leeward; but I could not help looking with still greater interest at the Admiral, who, during all this time, was shaving himself with a composure that quite astonished me.'

Once on deck, and now under fire, the admiral continued to maintain an air of nonchalance – that unflinching disregard for danger under fire, deliberately assumed to encourage a sense of order in an atmosphere of noise, confusion and death – so often recorded in the eyewitness accounts of this period. Smith went on to relate how Collingwood spoke calmly to him in the middle of the action and again for a few minutes at its conclusion: '... on neither occasion could I observe the slightest change from his ordinary manner. This ... made an impression on me which will never be effaced ... I wondered how a person whose mind was occupied by such a variety of most important concerns could, with the utmost ease and equanimity, inquire kindly after my welfare, and talk of common matters as if nothing of consequence was taking place.'

If successful in action, an admiral was expected to pursue and destroy the enemy's remaining vessels with as much vigour as circumstances would permit, or face criticism for failing to do so, as did Lord Howe after the battle of the Glorious First of June in 1794. If, on the other hand, he were defeated, he was to save as many of his vessels as possible and assist those of his ships that were disabled and therefore vulnerable to capture. If, in the immediate wake of battle, he were pleased with the conduct of his subordinates, it was customary for him to recognize this publicly by issuing a general order of thanks to the respective captains of his fleet or squadron. It of course also fell to the admiral to report regularly to the Admiralty, particularly in the immediate wake of a general engagement. A dispatch did not need to be lengthy, but at a minimum included a brief narrative of the action, a list of the ships engaged on both sides, comments on those officers worthy of distinction – it was not yet naval practice to highlight the conduct of individual seaman by name – and a list of casualties, known as a return, including an estimate of enemy losses.

Lieutenants and midshipmen killed in action or who subsequently died as a result of their wounds before reaching landfall were buried at sea in a ceremony conducted by the captain, unless in the heat of battle their bodies had been flung over the side to prevent encumbering the deck, as was the case for ordinary seamen. The bodies of captains and admirals were not cast into the sea during action, but rather buried at sea or returned home in a cask of brandy or other alcoholic preservative for eventual burial on land. Government support for widows of lieutenants, captains and admirals came in the form of that officer's full year's pay, with orphans receiving a third of that amount,

Rear Admiral Sir Horatio Nelson and a party of sailors from the *Theseus* in close-quarter fighting against a Spanish boat during the blockade of Cadiz in 1797. Notwithstanding his senior rank, Nelson always thrust himself into the forefront of danger, thus leading by example – the very foundation of good officership. (Author's collection)

Nelson being treated for a head wound aboard HMS *Vanguard* at the battle of the Nile, August 1798. A midshipman stands behind the rear admiral while two lieutenants are also present: one kneeling with scalpel in hand, and to centre rear with a bandaged head. The officer standing with two epaulettes is a lieutenant of Marines. (Stratford Archive)

unless they were married, in which case they were not eligible for any assistance. If the officer were unmarried, his mother could claim her share as if she were his widow, but only providing she too were a widow and over 50. If he were wounded, with the loss of an eye or limb, or the complete loss of the use of a limb, he received a full year's pay and could charge reasonable medical expenses to the Navy, providing he had a certificate from the Surgeons' Company in London.

Admirals perceived to have failed in their duties in the face of the enemy were subject to the disapprobation of their seniors or, worse still, of the Admiralty – or indeed both – a circumstance that befell Admiral Lord Cochrane in 1809 when, after conducting his celebrated fireship attack at Aix Roads, he publicly criticized his indecisive superior, Admiral James

H **OFFICERS AND MIDSHIPMEN IN ACTION ON THE QUARTERDECK OF A FLAGSHIP**

In the foreground, the admiral (**1**), shown as Collingwood would have looked at Trafalgar, shouts instructions in the midst of battle. In the background, the mortally wounded ship's captain (**2**), in the style of full dress uniform worn by many of the captains at Trafalgar – with long lapels with ten loops each, cuff lace and three-button cuff flaps – is supported by the first lieutenant (**3**), dressed in dark blue coat with a double row of gold buttons, white pantaloons and knee-high black boots. Behind the admiral stands a midshipman (**4**) noting down the ship's position and recording the signals to be hoisted for the benefit of the fleet. The ships' company busy themselves either working the rigging (**5**) or 'fighting' (i.e. crewing) – as contemporaries called it – the guns (**6**). When an enemy vessel came within effective musket range – under 50 yards – Marines (**7**) added small-arms fire to the storm of round, canister and grape shot unleashed by the ship's 18-, 24-, and 36-pdrs.

In unusual cases, an officer's appointment was merely temporary, with that rank relinquished when the particular appointment came to an end. Thus, a post captain might receive a temporary appointment in command of a small number of ships, with the rank of commodore, flying a special pennant to designate that status. In the case of vessels smaller than a frigate, particularly of sloops and brigs, the senior officer was a lieutenant, but in light of his responsibility for the entire vessel held the provisional rank of 'master and commander', or in its shortened form, 'commander'. A lieutenant was naturally keen to hold this post, for it enabled him to demonstrate his abilities in independent command. However, he gave up the title once he was recalled to his own ship or placed on half pay. Another temporary rank, that of sub-lieutenant, was introduced in 1804 to provide a lieutenant in command of a sloop or brig with more officers, especially for watch keeping. In such cases, he was assigned a second master, responsible for navigation, and a deserving senior midshipman who held the temporary rank of sub-lieutenant.

Gambier, for which impertinence Cochrane was hauled before a court martial. Dismissed from the service, he took command of several fledgling national navies in South America before being restored to the Royal Navy in 1831 as a rear admiral. Calling into question the conduct of a senior officer sometimes came with a price, if not always deserved. Rear Admiral Nelson himself, whilst serving as second-in-command under Admiral Sir Hyde Parker in the Baltic campaign of 1801, would not have escaped a court martial for failing to obey his superior's signal at the battle of Copenhagen to withdraw from action had he not already enjoyed a distinguished reputation on the basis of his conduct at the Nile and defeated the Danish fleet on the occasion in question, albeit at heavy cost to his own force.

Midshipmen and officers who performed particularly well in battle were eligible for promotion, or some other distinction in the case of officers only, such as a knighthood, peerage or further elevation within the peerage. In 1798, for instance, Parliament not only raised Nelson to the peerage as Baron Nelson of the Nile, but voted him a pension of £2,000 per annum. In addition, the King of Naples conferred on him the title Duke of Bronte. Recognition need not be confined to Government or foreign courts, however; individuals and organizations occasionally rewarded admirals whom they regarded as especially deserving. After the battle of the Nile, all ranks aboard the squadron presented a sword to Nelson, while credit for the most extraordinary gift of them all must surely fall to Captain Benjamin Hallowell who, in May 1799, sent Nelson the macabre present of a coffin fashioned out of the mainmast of the French flagship *Orient*, remarking in the accompanying letter, 'that when you are tired of this Life you may be buried in one of your own Trophies – but may that period be far distant, is the sincere wish of your obedient and much obliged servant.' Nelson was flattered by the gift, which served the purpose for which it was intended in January 1806 when the admiral's body was interred within a larger sarcophagus in the crypt of St Paul's Cathedral.

MUSEUMS AND PLACES OF INTEREST

Those interested in sites relating to the officers and midshipmen of the Royal Navy during the French Revolutionary and Napoleonic Wars are encouraged to visit the Royal Naval Museum at Portsmouth, Hampshire, which houses a large collection of naval artefacts, weapons, uniforms and paintings, not merely of Nelson's day, but spanning the era from early modern times to the present day. No visit would be complete, however, without an examination of HMS *Victory*, Nelson's flagship at Trafalgar, which sits splendidly preserved in dry dock opposite the museum. Much can be learned of the lives of British officers and midshipmen through an examination of this vessel, above all Nelson's stateroom and private quarters, Captain Hardy's cabin, the lieutenants' cubicles and the midshipmen's berth on the orlop deck. Walking the quarterdeck, moreover, will provide insight into the problems of command and control aboard a ship of the line, while the narrowness and low beams of the gun decks impressively reveal the confines in which midshipmen worked during battle.

Nelson on the quarterdeck of the *Victory* at Trafalgar, together with Captain Hardy (beside him with telescope) and several of the ship's lieutenants. Those dressed in scarlet jackets are Marines. (Stratford Archive)

The National Maritime Museum at Greenwich, south-west London, is an indispensable stop for those seeking to deepen their knowledge of the officers and midshipmen of the Nelsonian navy. Quite apart from the thousands of objects and images relating to British maritime history, the Nelson Gallery alone justifies a visit. The Chatham Historic Dockyard in Kent and Buckler's Hard in Hampshire offer interesting insights into not only the construction of warships of the age of sail, but conditions aboard such vessels, particularly ships of the line. Much can be gleaned about life aboard frigates of the era by visiting HMS *Trincomalee*, which, although post-dating the Napoleonic Wars by two years, follows the same design of her predecessors. The oldest ship afloat in Britain, *Trincomalee* is situated in the Historic Quay in Hartlepool, County Durham.

BIBLIOGRAPHY AND FURTHER READING

Adkin, Mark, *The Trafalgar Companion: The Guide to History's Most Famous Sea Battle and the Life of Admiral Lord Nelson* Aurum Press: London, 2005

Blake, Nicholas, *Steering to Glory: A Day in the Life of a Ship of the Line* Chatham Publishing: London, 2005

Blake, Nicholas, and Richard Lawrence, *The Illustrated Companion to Nelson's Navy* Chatham Publishing: London, 1999

Clayton, Tim, *Tars: The Men Who Made Britain Rule the Waves* Hodder & Stoughton: London, 2007

Fabb, John, and Jack Cassin-Scott, *The Uniforms of Trafalgar* B. T. Batsford: London, 1977

Falconer, William, and William Burney, *Falconer's Universal Dictionary of the Marine* Chatham Publishing: London, orig. ed. 1815; reprinted 2003

Fremont-Barnes, Gregory, Battle Orders 31: *The Royal Navy 1793–1815* Osprey Publishing Ltd: Oxford, 2007

——, Campaign 157: *Trafalgar 1805* Osprey Publishing Ltd: Oxford, 2005

——, Duel 9: *Victory vs Redoutable: Ships of the Line at Trafalgar 1805* Osprey Publishing Ltd: Oxford, 2008

——, Warrior 100: *Nelson's Sailors* Osprey Publishing Ltd: Oxford, 2005

Goodwin, Peter, *Men O'War: The Illustrated Story of Life in Nelson's Navy* National Maritime Museum: London, 2004

Haythornthwaite, Philip, Elite 48: *Nelson's Navy* Osprey Publishing Ltd: Oxford, 1999

Henderson, James, *Frigates, Sloops and Brigs* Leo Cooper: London, 2005

King, Dean, and John B. Hattendorf, *Every Man Will Do His Duty: An Anthology of Firsthand Accounts from the Age of Nelson* Henry Holt & Co.: New York, 1997

Lavery, Brian, *Jack Aubrey Commands: An Historical Companion to the Naval World of Patrick O'Brian* Conway Maritime Press: London, 1997

——, *Nelson's Navy: The Ships, Men, and Organisation, 1793–1815* Conway Maritime Press: London, 1992

——, *Shipboard Life and Organisation, 1731–1815* Ashgate: London, 1999

Lewis, Jon E. (ed.), *The Mammoth Book of How it Happened: Trafalgar* Robinson: London, 2005

——, (ed.), *The Mammoth Book of Life Before the Mast* Robinson: London, 2001

Lewis, Michael A., *A Social History of the Navy, 1793–1815* George Allen & Unwin: London, 1960

Masefield, John, *Sea Life in Nelson's Time* Conway Maritime Press: London, 1971

Maynard, C. (ed.), *A Nelson Companion: A Guide to the Royal Navy of Jack Aubrey* Michael O'Mara Books: London, 2004

Miller, David, *The World of Jack Aubrey: Twelve Pounders, Frigates, Cutlasses and Insignia of His Majesty's Royal Navy* Perseus Books: Jackson, TN, 2003

Miller, Nathan, *Broadsides: The Age of Fighting Sail, 1775–1815* John Wiley & Sons: London, 2001

Mosert, Noel, *The Line Upon a Wind: An Intimate History of the Last and Greatest War Fought at Sea under Sail, 1793–1815* Vintage: London, 2008

O'Neill, Richard, *Patrick O'Brian's Navy: The Illustrated Companion to Jack Aubrey's World* Running Press: Philadelphia, 2003

Pocock, Tom, *Trafalgar: An Eyewitness History* Penguin: London, 2005

Pope, Dudley, *Life in Nelson's Navy* Chatham Publishing: London, 1997

Pope, Stephen, *Hornblower's Navy: Life at Sea in the Age of Nelson* Welcome Rain: New York, 1998

Rodger, N. A. M., *The Command of the Ocean: A Naval History of Britain, 1649–1815* Penguin: London, 2006

——, *The Wooden World: Anatomy of the Georgian Navy* Fontana: London, 1988

Wareham, Tom, *Frigate Commander* Leo Cooper: London, 2004

——, *The Star Captains: Frigate Command in the Napoleonic Wars* Chatham Publishing: London, 2003

Warwick, Peter, *Voices from the Battle of Trafalgar* David & Charles: Newton Abbot, 2006

INDEX